Curiocities

Where Complex Cities Meet Curious Minds

Other World Scientific Title by the Author

COMversations: Communication Lessons from Media Professionals
ISBN: 978-981-125-352-2
ISBN: 978-981-125-370-6 (pbk)

Curiocities

Where Complex Cities Meet Curious Minds

Chua Chong Jin

Nanyang Technological University, Singapore

Introduction by

Jason Pomeroy

Pomeroy Studio, Singapore

NEW JERSEY · LONDON · SINGAPORE · BEIJING · SHANGHAI · HONG KONG · TAIPEI · CHENNAI · TOKYO

Published by

World Scientific Publishing Co. Pte. Ltd.

5 Toh Tuck Link, Singapore 596224

USA office: 27 Warren Street, Suite 401-402, Hackensack, NJ 07601

UK office: 57 Shelton Street, Covent Garden, London WC2H 9HE

Library of Congress Control Number: 2022034358

British Library Cataloguing-in-Publication Data
A catalogue record for this book is available from the British Library.

CURIOCITIES
Where Complex Cities Meet Curious Minds

Copyright © 2023 by Chong Jin Chua

ISBN 978-981-126-502-0 (hardcover)
ISBN 978-981-126-561-7 (paperback)
ISBN 978-981-126-503-7 (ebook for institutions)
ISBN 978-981-126-504-4 (ebook for individuals)

For any available supplementary material, please visit
https://www.worldscientific.com/worldscibooks/10.1142/13106#t=suppl

Desk Editor: Lai Ann

Typeset by Diacritech Technologies Pvt. Ltd.
Chennai - 600106, India

To dearest Jean whose savvy mix of fuss and flow has led us to
cities near and far

To dad whose encyclopaedias brought the world home for me –
right into our HDB rental flat

To mum …. hardly a traveller, yet so vastly open in spirit

Most of all, to God for his protection – seen and unseen –
amidst all movements

ABOUT THE TEAM

CHUA CHONG JIN

A former Straits Times journalist and Asia correspondent for PHP International (Japan), **Chong Jin** teaches at Nanyang Business School at the Nanyang Technological University, Singapore. Educated at the National University of Singapore and Cambridge University in UK, he is intrigued by diversity – of people, places and practices.

JASON POMEROY

An award-winning architect, **Jason** is also an academic, author and TV host. The founder of sustainable design firm Pomeroy Studio and sustainable educator Pomeroy Academy, he has a master's degree from Cambridge University and a PhD from the University of Westminster. As a TV host, his works include City Time Traveller, City Redesign and Smart Cities 2.0 for Channel News Asia.

ULRIKE MURFETT

A consultant in higher education specialising in management communication and presentations, **Ulrike** taught for many years in a tertiary institution in Singapore. With an MA from Karl-Franzens-Universität, Graz, Austria, the award-winning educator has also written and edited academic textbooks and has worked as a translator of technical and medical texts.

CONTENTS

Acknowledgements

This book started with a yearning that was all too familiar during those travel-starved days in 2021. Like others, I could not get out of the country during the pandemic. I missed the many wonderful things about travelling, including good food and the chance to meet people in diverse cities.

The withdrawal was getting to me. One way to cope was to link up with those whose careers have taken them to places and hear their stories. I must truly thank the 10 people featured in *Curiocities: Where Complex Cities Meet Curious Minds* for their time and support. They include veteran diplomat/ author/professor Kishore Mahbubani, poet/author/brand consultant Koh Buck Song, India correspondent Debarshi Dasgupta, East Asia specialist and TV correspondent Maria Siow, and Japan correspondent Walter Sim.

The other five are novelist/lecturer Balli Kaur Jaswal, documentary photographer Edwin Koo, Malaysia bureau chief Shannon Teoh, travel writer/editor Clara Chow and novelist/diplomat Warran Kalasegaran. As revealed in their own words in the chapters that follow, sparks fly when complex cities meet curious minds.

Special thanks go to Dr Jason Pomeroy, the founder of sustainable design firm Pomeroy Studio and sustainable educator Pomeroy Academy. An architect, academic, author and TV host, he is known for his ardent love for cities all over the world – and this is reflected in his Introduction for the book.

Then there is my former colleague and friend Ulrike Murfett who kindly stepped in to help me with the piece on Balli Kaur after I did the interview. Obviously helpful are old contacts – like Chua Hong Koon, Publishing Director of World Scientific Publishing, for instance – whose support has made this project possible. Thanks too to my wife Jeannette Xavier and desk editor Lai Ann for editing a large part of the text and Chennai-based company diacriTech for the design of the book.

Finally, I am grateful for the indulgence of the people around me, especially friends, family members, colleagues and students. Often they graciously accept me for who I am, including my tendency to dream of "lands far far away".

BEAUTY OF WRITING

"Travel books, like others, change perspective as we grow older, and I can see now that Freya Stark's Ionia: A Quest *is an enchanting but disturbingly moralistic account of a journey that this remarkable woman took in the early 1950s along the west coast of Turkey. In those days these ancient Greek cities were virtually unvisited. In 55 sites Stark encountered only one other tourist. Relying largely on the witness of ancient writers, she mused among the ruins, deducing their cities' character from them as if the stones themselves might speak. It all sounds too dreadful. But such was the beauty of her writing, and the delicacy of her thought, that the result is captivating. It persuaded me, at the start of my career, how richly landscape and history may interfuse, and how deeply (and sometimes dangerously) a quiet attention can fire the imagination."*

COLIN THUBRON ON *IONIA: A QUEST* BY FREYA STARK

Source: The Guardian

HERITAGE OF PLACES

Picture courtesy of Jason Pomeroy

"My curiosity is piqued especially with regard to the architectural heritage of places. I continue to be amazed at how architecture can be used as a symbol of control, opulence and power. One sees this in the Spanish colonial fortifications of Intramuros in Manila; in the expression of the British Raj's decadence in the Oberoi in Kolkata; in the glistening skyscrapers of Shanghai that stand as testimony to China's economic reform. Yes, this is what successful places do to us – they leave an indelible mark in our minds. Like the Ancient Mariner *in Coleridge's famous poem, we are then moved to share constantly with others to keep the stories alive."*

—Jason Pomeroy

To All The Cities I Love

Jason Pomeroy
Professor/Architect/TV Host

Pictures courtesy of Jason Pomeroy

I have a passion for places, peoples and cultures. This may be due in part to my background – my cross-cultural heritage and the way I was brought up. I was born in the UK to a British father and a Malaysian-Chinese mother. That – in my case at least – paved the way for what some may call a peripatetic lifestyle. As a child, I was flitting between London and the occasional European city. Then there were the summer months in Malaysia, particularly the cities of Taiping, Penang and Kuala Lumpur where the tropical heat and humidity was a welcome break from the cold and temperate.

Those early days planted in me a fascination with the diversity of places, peoples and practices – a fascination that has only grown stronger, given the duality of my daily life as an architect and academic. Things have a way of coming full circle – like what happened when I did my first and post-graduate degrees in architecture at the Canterbury School of Architecture – between 1992 and 1995 and then between 1997 and 1998. It was during this period that I was drawn to the study of Asian cities (in particular Hong Kong, Kuala Lumpur and Singapore). I was struck by how they could salvage open space for social amenity and recreation while retaining low carbon footprints.

Between 1995 and 1996, I did a placement as a designer in between my degrees at the firm of Pakatan Reka Architects in Kuala Lumpur. It led me to appreciate the role that local culture, historical precedents, topography and climate could play in the design of the built environment. I learnt much from the design works of Charles Correa and Ken Yeang as well as from the writings of Kenneth Frampton – people who would become my early influences in critical regionalist architecture.

This was followed by a more traditional posting which led me to London as an architect with Yorke, Rosenberg and Mardell (YRM) in London, UK, in 1998. After two years, I made a cultural shift, so to speak, joining Japanese architecture, engineering, construction and development corporation, Kajima. Working in Brussels, London and Amsterdam, this was a fruitful five-year period. It was during this time that I started to develop an interest in interdisciplinary design and in particular how a sustainable collaborative process can deliver a sustainable product that safeguards quality, minimises cost and reduces waste.

Between 2002 and 2005, led by my interest in the sustainability of the construction process, I pursued a master's degree in Interdisciplinary Design for the Built Environment (IDBE) at the University of Cambridge. I did my thesis entitled, "The skycourt: an alternative social space for the 21st century", which would become an important vein of research for me and further influence my design projects.

Editor's Note: *The thesis would serve as a base for his book "The Skycourt and Skygarden: Greening the Urban Habitat" as well as his PhD from the University of Westminster which he obtained in 2015.*

Meanwhile, foreign cities beckoned, even as I was comfortably settled (or so I thought) in familiar Europe again. I had joined the London office of the architecture, urbanism and design firm Broadway Malyan in 2005. An opportunity arose and I was relocated to Singapore in 2007 to establish its presence here, with active involvement in shaping cities like Kuala Lumpur, Jakarta and Manila. Singapore has remained my base since and, in 2012, I started my sustainable urbanism, architecture, design, and research firm Pomeroy Studio.

I am also the Founder of sustainability educator, Pomeroy Academy. Which is why, apart from my business, I also set aside time for both teaching and media work. I didn't quite plan it so meticulously but this arrangement has somehow deepened my lifelong link to global cities. Teaching, for instance, has opened doors for work at places like the University of Cambridge and the University of Nottingham in UK, Universita IUAV di Venezia in Italy and James Cook University in Australia. At the same time, I continue to promote aspects of urbanism and sustainability at international conferences and events, including TEDx and the World Architecture Festival. Even more serendipitously perhaps, I have had the privilege of introducing some of the world's most fascinating cities to the masses through the power of broadcast media in the interests of raising awareness of the cultural role architecture and the built environment can play in society.

Most memorably for me, I appreciate the opportunity to be both consultant and host of the architecture/travel TV series *City Time Traveller* by Channel News Asia in 2014 and 2015. It was such a privilege to explore so many cities in so many countries in such an intense, time-sensitive fashion. The energy, intensity and uniqueness of each place can be both overwhelming and humbling as one attunes to the pulse of its time-tested cultural practices. This is true whether one is talking about the Hindu rituals on the river Ganges in Varanasi or the ancient tea ceremony in Kyoto. Awe inspiring too is that sense of the spectacular – be it the skyline from the pinnacle of the Birds Nest in Beijing or the ancient ruins of Wat Chai Wattanaram in Ayutthaya. Off the beaten track, the curious minded is often richly rewarded. My curiosity is piqued especially with regard to the architectural heritage of places. I continue to be amazed at how architecture can be used as a symbol of control, opulence and power. One sees this in the Spanish colonial fortifications of Intramuros in Manila; in the expression of the British Raj's decadence in the Oberoi in Kolkata; in the glistening skyscrapers of Shanghai that stand as testimony to China's economic reform. Yes, this is what successful places do to us – they leave an indelible mark in our minds. Like the *Ancient Mariner* in Coleridge's famous poem, we are then moved to share constantly with others to keep the stories alive.

Since *City Time Traveller*, I have gone on to do other shows focusing on cities. I have explored, for instance, how smart cities may be perceived as technology-centric habitats of futuristic innovations but are equally a lesson in mankind's pursuit of culture, innovation and social purpose, making them livable and lovable. It is always a journey of discovery and one inevitably comes away both enriched and humbled. With an open mind and a thirst to pursue the truth and meaning behind our built environment creations (and thus our very existence), one can learn endlessly. About how Barcelona puts the technology into the hands of those who want to make the lives of their fellow citizens smoother while retaining Catalan cultural heritage. About how Bandung in Indonesia leverages people power and social media to get smarter. About how the Smart City quest of Japan's Higashimatsushima, born out of tragedy, will allow it to become truly self-sufficient and resilient to future climate change-related cataclysms.

Other tales await the curious – whether one is looking at Songdo in South Korea; Shenzhen in China; Ahmedabad in India; Amsterdam in The Netherlands; or Singapore. I am so thankful to have been initiated into the intricacies of these complex cities even as I continue to enjoy the places I have been most exposed to – such as London and Venice. London – where I was born, raised and once worked – continually captivates through its heritage, idiosyncrasy and eccentricity. The Roman ruins in the old city; the captivating street and market culture; the Baroque geometries of St Paul's Cathedral; the sheer audacity of 'The Shard' – there is much to like. Meanwhile, Venice – an epicentre for trade, commerce and culture for centuries – displays the vestiges of its former glory through the preservation of architectural masterpieces that is like a living, breathing "urban museum" of nostalgia. To this day, in these travel-deprived times, I yearn for a return to my favourite haunts in these cities.

I have told my story – in particular my love for places – for the Introduction of this new book, *Curiocities: Where Complex Cities Meet Curious Minds*. Mine is just one person's account of the appeal of cities and how they have a way of drawing you into worlds unknown. What holds true for me must certainly be so too – perhaps in different ways – for the 10 colourful personalities featured in this collection. Each has a unique tale of his or her own. Reading their accounts put together by author Chua Chong Jin, my sense is their lives have been enriched by their exposure to diverse cities and experiences. And often, it is their sense of curiosity and their willingness to embrace the complexities of peoples, places and practices that have helped them not only survive but thrive. Below are glimpses of their stories:

KISHORE MAHBUBANI: His is one of the first names to surface when we think of someone who has been highly globalised and exposed to cities of the world. The veteran diplomat, university professor and author of influential titles like *Can Asians Think?*, *The New Asian Hemisphere*, *The Great Convergence*, *Can Singapore Survive?*, *Has the West Lost It?* and *Has China Won?* has had postings in Malaysia, Cambodia and USA where he was based in Washington and New York. There is much that can be mined from his rich experiences professionally and intellectually. Yet sometimes the best and the most poignant insights relate to ordinary, day-to-day encounters. Like those he has shared in this book. Recalling his days abroad, he notes: "I would say the wonderful thing about living in different cities is that each city has its own character and identity. So it's a joy to discover the identity of each city. For example, I remember one time I was taking a taxi in New York. My driver happened to be a migrant from Sweden. When he heard that I studied Philosophy in Singapore, we had a very deep and intense discussion of Western philosophy. That to me was a great educational experience. Similarly there was another taxi driver I met in New York who wasn't wealthy but a lot of his earnings went to a school in India which was educating a few hundred young girls. I remember my youngest son – who was between 10 and 12 years old then – being very moved by the story. He insisted that I must tip this driver well. So whether it is London, Paris, Tokyo or any other city, one soon learns that each city has its unique cultural organism and it's a joy to actually discover the nature of that cultural organism."

KOH BUCK SONG: Through his book *Around The World In 68 Days*, a travelogue of sorts, poet/author/brand consultant Koh offers insights into ancient and modern cultures. He explores their national identities and nation brands, and their place in the world today. The book is a fascinating ride, "a type of memoir, a tribute to travel, of a pre-Covid-19 world" as he recalls visits to places like Panama, Okinawa and Madagascar. Along the way, he rewards readers with rich perspectives that can only come from curious explorations. "The world is so abundantly varied, but from the many cities I've been to, there are a few aspects that resonate most with me. One centres on places that are at the nexus, the interface, of two or more worlds, such as Istanbul, between Asia and Europe, or Morocco, between Africa and Europe. Such places are always a blend of myriad influences, and it's enriching to explore how diversity transforms – and usually enhances – the character of these societies. Another facet is the unique situation of small states, especially islands in strategic locations, or, sometimes, places surrounded by larger, troubled territories – from Singapore to Cuba or Costa Rica – that have been the focus of claims and contestations from internal and external influences throughout history. I'm always curious about how such societies cope with managing their internal challenges while opening up to engage with the world outside, such as keeping heritage and tradition afloat amidst the inexorable currents of modernity. A metaphor for this from my 68-day trip is how the turtles of Oman keep swimming against the ocean's waves, to clamber back to shore to nest every year," he notes eloquently.

DEBARSHI DASGUPTA: For India correspondent Dasgupta, who is based in New Delhi, the complexity of his country and its cities cannot be overemphasized. He says: "I don't want to oversimplify because if I did so, I would be dishonest to myself and disrespectful to my country's incredible diversity. I often tell foreigners it is best to think of India as an entity similar to the European Union with the states here - each with its own kind of politics, culture and language - resembling the diverse countries that comprise the EU. That's the kind of wide-angle view one has to adopt when looking at India from outside." Just as there is no Indian cuisine (there are many kinds of Indian cuisines), the adjective "Indian" hides more than it reveals, he adds. Citing an example, he notes: "For instance, Bollywood is often rendered as being synonymous with the Indian cinema industry. The term just refers to the Hindi film industry based in Mumbai and there are many other film industries that are based in different parts of the country, each with its own glorious traditions and millions of fans. It is worth remembering this inherent diversity when one starts to read and learn more about India. Don't get daunted by this thought; think of it in terms of how much more there is to explore than what meets the eye and enjoy India!"

MARIA SIOW: In the course of a rich career in journalism, mainly in broadcasting, Siow has lived in Hong Kong and Beijing as a foreign correspondent and studied in Seoul and Washington. Hers is an exemplary tale of constant learning through constant exposure – to new places, new challenges, new cultures. Guided by an enduring interest in East Asian history and culture, she shows what it means to be always on the move in one's quest to keep growing. With years on the ground in China, she offers intriguing stories about this vast country but remains humbled by its complexity. Asked what continues to fascinate her and keep her curious, she says, offering some prized insider's perspective: "Some of the more intriguing places to me are usually the border cities that China shares with countries that it has a common border with. Dongxing in Guangxi province, which borders Vietnam, is intriguing and feels very Southeast Asian to me. Apart from Chinese, signs are also written in Vietnamese and Southeast Asian products can easily be purchased here. Or Suifenhe in Heilongjiang province, which shares a common border with Russia, where you can easily buy Russian dolls, breads and vodka. Signs too are also written partly in Russian. Or Hunchun in Jilin province, which is the place to go to for a taste of both Russian and North Korean cultures/influences."

SHANNON TEOH: Based in Kuala Lumpur as Malaysia bureau chief, Teoh reminds us anew about the need to go beyond simplistic depictions based on surface familiarity. Taking the example of foreigners' encounter with Malaysia, he notes how many make no effort to understand the differences among states. Instead, they fall back simply on stereotypes surrounding familiar places like Johor, Penang, Malacca and Kuala Lumpur. Making a case for the diversity of states (a reality which is often overlooked), he cites some compelling examples. "Kelantan is fiercely different from everywhere else, including neighbouring Terengganu. It has less beautiful seasides and greenery. While being the so-called most Islamist state, its own ancestral beliefs are also the most intriguing in Malaysia. Perak is a beautiful balance of old and new. Melaka and Negri Sembilan play host to various minorities and practices that tell of a deep history whose continuity was broken by colonialism." His bigger point is that neat categories are a sort of administrative convenience. So his advice for the curious minded is this: "Speak to people, visit their shops and homes, and you will find there is no real 'Malay' or 'Chinese' or 'Indian' family, but rather subdivisions upon subdivisions. These are just colonial constructs being carried forward and in fact deepened by the establishment to ease its own work of keeping on top of things."

CLARA CHOW: For author Chow, her role as a creative writer has opened some global doors – with the opportunity to be writer-in-residence at places like the University of Iowa (USA), Toji Cultural Centre (South Korea), Bogong Centre of Sound Culture (Australia) and Rimbun Dahan (Malaysia). On her various stints, she says: "I'm very grateful for being able to go on residencies and spend time in the company of other writers and readers, and learn from them. Every chance to go somewhere new has taught me so much and changed me in fundamental ways. Each opportunity is so different. Toji was the first residency I did, and it completely changed my life, in the sense that I realised to be a writer is to live a life of discipline, determination and patience, which has nothing to do with external validation or financial reward. (In the case of) Rimbun Dahan, spending a month solo in a little garage-converted-to-house in Selangor jungle taught me that I was braver than I thought." Yet, even as she learns more, she – in the spirit of true curiosity – feels ever more keenly what she doesn't know. As she puts it succinctly: "Making my way through the world, I try not to essentialise, so I really couldn't say what I've learnt about people collectively as nations compared to people I know in Singapore."

EDWIN KOO: For award-winning documentary photographer Koo, curiosity takes on added depth when it is guided by a strong sense of personal conviction about one's craft. Stressing the importance of long-term personal projects, he explains: "Photographs are great at conveying emotions.

Photographs are very truthful in this aspect because they transport you across time and space to experience viscerally a nugget of history. But this experience is filtered differently in different people. So is a photograph fact? Yes. Is experiencing a photograph fiction? Yes! Because we 'imagine' what it was like and are informed by our own biases. That is why it is important to make long term personal projects – time distills the truth, and the truth is not one moment but a continuum. A substantial number of well-taken photographs, curated properly in a thoughtful manner, is capable of giving us a rather truthful account of history, no matter how subjective the photography is." In his case, his quest led him to unexplored themes in places like Nepal and Pakistan. "While in Nepal, I focused on the local themes that appealed to me – Maoist insurgency and Tibetan refugees. These were also themes that appealed to international publications, so the stars aligned. Of course, I delved into other projects but, in the end, these were the ones that held my attention. Even till now, I continue to find them intriguing." He also had an opportunity to travel to Pakistan in 2009. It was there that he started what he would consider his most important work to date – *Paradise*. In essence, it is about a paradisical place called Swat Valley which fell prey to both man-made and natural tragedies.

WALTER SIM: Based in Tokyo as foreign correspondent to cover Japan, Sim is well served by his sense of curiosity and appetite for new adventures. As he notes: "It is exciting to find a new rhythm to life in an entirely different country and to practise my Japanese while making mistakes along the way. As a bonus, there is the joy of travelling and finding places off the beaten track. The way many things are done in Japan will bewilder any fresh-eyed Singaporean – and that was me at first. Indeed, the dissonance was especially great in my first few months. It is once again amplified during the Covid-19 pandemic when I have been stupefied by many things." Indeed, even as he learns new things all the time, he is keenly aware of what he doesn't know yet despite having a ringside seat in a dynamic society that is at odds with modernity and tradition. Still, there is for him that sense of wonder from understanding in some depth how complex the country is. He explains: "Japan comprises 47 prefectures, all of which are individually larger in size than Singapore. It is a fallacy to equate Japan to Tokyo. Every region has its own characteristics, heritage, food, dialect, culture and even local government. This also gives rise to very different issues in different prefectures and cities," he says, citing how diverse localised issues shape places like Hokkaido, Fukushima, Kyoto, Okinawa, Yokohama and Niigata.

BALLI KAUR: Born in Singapore, novelist Kaur grew up all over the world and has lived in countries like Japan, Russia, Turkey, the United States, Australia and the Philippines. So curiosity is a sort of doubled edged sword for her. She is curious about the many worlds she has been exposed to. At the same time, she has had to manage the curiosity others have about her each time she lands in a new place. Recalling her early years, she says: "My father worked for the Singapore Foreign Ministry, which meant that we lived in many different countries and experienced different cultures. This has certainly shaped my identity. Moving around, I was always on the outside, never truly belonging." So she developed a strong inner world, with books and stories providing consistency. From a young age, she needed narratives to explain the complexities of her background. "I am Singaporean, but from the Punjabi Sikh community. People I met did not always know that Singapore is multicultural. They thought of Singapore as being somewhere in China or even as a Chinese country (whatever that meant to them). So, with the way I look and all, I did not really fit into their preconceptions....Then, whenever we came back to Singapore from a posting abroad, I (also) had to justify my claim about being Singaporean.... (As) a Punjabi Sikh, I am from a small minority within a minority group in Singapore, so I did not attend Tamil classes or celebrate Deepavali. These nuances also needed to be explained. Responding to questions about my identity necessitated stories that helped to illustrate who I am, and that was probably good training for a writer."

WARRAN KALASEGARAN: Through his education, Warran, who has been working at the Ministry of Foreign Affairs since 2016 and is currently based in Kuala Lumpur, has had the opportunity to be exposed to cities like Warwick in UK and Tokyo in Japan. He also had valuable internship experiences in places like New York, Jakarta, Seoul and Geneva. On what being based in another place – with its unique cultures and mores – means to him, he notes: "It is the differences among us that make the world colourful and interesting. I enjoy learning about how different places and communities developed different architecture or foods or political systems over time, and soaking in different experiences. This could be walking through the red Akamon gate to enter Tokyo University, trying durians in Pahang, or visiting Shakespeare's home near Warwick University and learning about the words he coined. Most of all, I like meeting people who come from different backgrounds, hearing their stories, and making friends. Eventually, it is that sense of friendship that no longer makes a place feel different or 'other', but makes you feel like you could belong too." Citing his stint in Japan as an example to show the warmth of human ties and the importance of embracing – and being embraced by – a community, he recalls: "When I moved (there), learning a martial art was on my bucket list. I like sports and I wanted to try a Japanese activity. There was a *dojo* near my home that taught *kudo*, a combination of karate and judo. Neither the instructor nor most of the students spoke English. At my first class, a senior student gestured to me to change into gym clothes. But as I was already changed, I misinterpreted him and took my shirt off! I started learning by watching my instructor and following his moves. Eventually, the first Japanese words I learned were about decimating someone – kick (*keri*), front kick (*mae keri*), knee (*hiza*). But I got to know my teammates better over the two years. At my first fight, they were at my corner, helping me warm up and encouraging me throughout the fight. I felt proud for learning a new skill. But given how much of an adjustment moving to Japan was, I felt even happier for finding a community."

Ten curious minds. Ten different stories featuring unique encounters with people, places and practices. Together, the personalities featured all share one distinctive practice – the art of documenting their experiences through journalistic pieces, novels, photography, travel books or influential books covering topics like the rise of Asia, Singapore's future and US-China relations. The value of such expression – in whatever form – is captured succinctly by renowned travel writer Pico Iyer. "Writing of every kind is a way to wake oneself up and keep as alive as when one has just fallen in love," he notes. If this is so, and I believe it is, I can only welcome yet another labour of love (what book isn't in our fast-paced age?) to all the cities I love – and the curious minds they tenderly elicit.

LABOUR OF LOVE

Picture courtesy of Jason Pomeroy

"Together, the personalities featured in Curiocities *all share one distinctive practice: the art of documenting their experiences – through journalistic pieces, novels, photography, travel books or influential books covering topics like the rise of Asia, Singapore's future and US-China relations. The value of such expression – in whatever form – is captured succinctly by renowned travel writer Pico Iyer. 'Writing of every kind is a way to wake oneself up and keep as alive as when one has just fallen in love,' he notes. If this is so, and I believe it is, I can only welcome yet another labour of love (what book isn't in our fast-paced age?) to all the cities I love – and the curious minds they tenderly elicit."*

—Jason Pomeroy

BREATHTAKING PROSE

"When Bruce Chatwin died in 1989, at 48, he had published just five books: a small yet dazzling output. His first, In Patagonia, is a metaphysical exploration of 'the uttermost part of the earth'. It is in the eyes of many his best, though it was not his most commercially successful (Songlines outsold it many times over). But it is probably the most influential travel book written since the war. Its opening page – telling of Bruce's childhood discovery of a piece of dinosaur skin in his grandmother's cupboard – is possibly the most imitated passage in modern travel literature. Chatwin had three matchless gifts: he was a thinker of genuine originality; a reader of astonishing erudition; and a writer of breathtaking prose. All three talents shine brightly on almost every page of In Patagonia, but it is his bleak chiselled prose that remains his most dazzling: he had a quite remarkable ability to evoke place, to bring to life a whole world of strange sounds and smells in a single unexpected image, to pull a perfect sentence out the air with the ease of a child netting a butterfly. The pendulum of fashion has swung against Chatwin, and it is now unhip to admire his work. Yet to his fans, Chatwin remains like a showy bird of paradise amid the sparrows of the present English literary scene, and it is impossible to reread In Patagonia without a deep stab of sadness that we have lost the brightest and most profound writer of his generation. He also knew and loved the Islamic world – and such writers are now badly in demand. God only knows what Chatwin might have produced had he still been writing, now when we need him most."

WILLIAM DALRYMPLE ON *IN PATAGONIA* BY BRUCE CHATWIN

Source: The Guardian

WHEN I WAS YOUNG

Picture courtesy of Kishore Mahbubani

"When I was young, all we aspired to as young people was to go to London, New York, Paris or one of the other great Western cities. Looking back at my early life, my love for these Western cities was understandable. I spent the first 15 years of my life, from 1948 to 1963, in a British colony. In a way, my generation was politically and mentally colonised. Growing up, we had the 'West is best' mindset. I once had a conversation with a primary school classmate who said he would like to go to London because its streets were paved with gold. But I think it's important for the young today to understand that the centre of gravity of the world's economy has now shifted to East Asia. It's no more in Europe. It's no more in America."

—Kishore Mahbubani

CHAPTER 1

When Love Beckons

Kishore Mahbubani
Diplomat/Author/Professor

Pictures courtesy of China Circle, Mothership, Assembly Series & Washington University of St. Louis

Professor Mahbubani, looking at your career, one of the things that stands out is the fact that you have had the privilege of two distinct careers – in diplomacy (1971 to 2004) and in academia (2004 to 2019). Broadly, what would you consider the best take aways from each chapter?

Well, I would say that I have learnt some hard truths. In diplomacy, I have learnt that the most important factor in international relations is power. Those who have power tend to be able to get their way. If there's a clash between power and principle, in theory, principle should be stronger and values should prevail. Yet power always trumps principle. Clearly, this is something that's quite surprising to the man in the street. People are often very surprised to learn that, at the end of the day, what really matters is power in international relations. In the case of academia, of course, I've learnt something quite different. It's about the power of ideas. If you have a good idea, even if you come from a small country, university or organisation, you can still have an impact. So broadly, these would be my main takeaways from my time in diplomacy and academia.

If I can just pick up on your point regarding the power of ideas. You speak about that with conviction. Can you share some personal examples which demonstrate clearly for you the power of ideas?

Well, if you look at my writing, I have written about the return of Asia on the global stage. In fact, that is basically the underlying theme of my nine books. That is an example of a central idea. People can be moved if you share with them a good idea. Personally, I appreciate the interest that even global intellectual giants like Lawrence Summers and Amartya Sen have shown whenever I share ideas with them. This is despite their busy schedules. For me, this affirms my belief that people will have time for you if you have good ideas to share. This shows me the value of exchanging ideas with others and that is why I continue to write books.

I find that to be true – the fact that people are drawn to good ideas. I'm just wondering: In a way, you are a personality yourself. So when you share your ideas, people might be drawn to them because you have a reputation and a record. I'm thinking about my undergraduates, for instance. They are young. People don't know them. So it's quite difficult for doors to open. **My question is: when you were much younger and just starting out, was this notion regarding the power of ideas indeed valid?**

Actually my whole writing career started as an undergraduate when I was studying Philosophy at the then University of Singapore. Those old enough may remember that I wrote an article once called "A Question of Decorum" which has been reproduced in my book, *Can Singapore Survive?* I was then a totally unknown undergraduate, yet the article got attention and I was interviewed by BBC and New York Times. In essence, that article was about an encounter between then Prime Minister Lee Kuan Yew and an undergraduate who was the chairman of a discussion session. I wrote an article about it and this generated much interest.

Just a very quick follow up. Some people may say all this was possible for you because you had a strong intellectual bent to begin with and was a President's Scholar. **Regarding the power of ideas, would you say it's confined to the elite or would you think it can be embraced in a wider manner by more people?**

Being President's Scholar didn't give me any special inroads into the world of ideas. For a start, getting it was a bonus for someone like me – with my humble background and all. Honestly when I finished Grade 12, or what you would call pre-university, I should have gone on to sell textiles on High Street, being the son of a Sindhi. And that was what happened indeed. After my studies at St. Andrew's School, I was earning $150 a month as a salesman in High Street. Then, from almost nowhere, came the President's Scholarship with its payment of $250 a month. Ever the practical person, my mother did the sums and decided that going to university on a scholarship made more sense. That was how I ended up in the University of Singapore.

What matters more, I think, is for you to go with your heart. Know what you are truly interested in though pursuing that over other things may come with a price. In my case, I enjoyed my four years at the Bukit Timah Campus in the University of Singapore because I pursued the subject I truly love – Philosophy. I stuck to my choice even though it meant repeating a year and giving up Economics and Sociology. In our pragmatic society, we think in terms of which subjects are practical and which are not. Well, I went for what many would consider an impractical subject and did well in it because I was passionate about it. I recall having some very inspiring teachers in the small Philosophy department at the university.

Editor's Note: Professor Mahbubani was awarded the President's Scholarship in 1967 and graduated with a First Class Honours degree in Philosophy from the University of Singapore in 1971.

Apart from these inspiring teachers, why Philosophy over other subjects?

It was a matter of comparison. In my Economics classes then, the notion of argument wasn't really there. Instead the focus was on memorisation and the so-called right answers. To me, there was a lack of debate and discussion. In contrast, in studying Philosophy, I felt liberated to discuss and examine issues with rigour without worrying about what the right answer or answers might be. That was how I started the intellectual journey of questioning. I would go to the library, look for the Philosophy section, pull out a book and spend hours reading. The fascinating ideas of Ludwig Wittgenstein, for example, would keep me very engaged and very entranced.

I think it was the poet W.B.Yeats who said that education is not about filling a bucket but lighting a fire. For me, the Economics department in my university at that time was trying to fill the bucket. In the Philosophy department, the focus was on lighting a fire. I told myself: "I prefer to have my brain on fire rather than have my brain full of water." That was how I ended up doing Philosophy and it was one of the best decisions I made in my life.

To me, if I hadn't done Philosophy, I wouldn't have been able to write as much as I have written. I'm trying to do a rough count. I may have published about a million words so far, and that would not have happened if I hadn't studied Philosophy. A lot of the titles of my books take the form of questions. That reflects my belief that it's the question that counts, not the answer.

Editor's Note: *For a glimpse of Professor Mahbubani's belief in raising probing questions, here is an extract from a piece he penned for The Straits Times in December 2021. Writing about what he calls the schizophrenia of Singapore, he notes: "Our economic veins are tied to the optimistic East, while our mental veins are tied to the pessimistic West. To resolve these contrasting tendencies in our minds, it may be useful to spend the year 2022 reflecting on where the long-term destiny of Singapore will be….. (My book Can Singapore Survive?) does not necessarily provide all the answers to Singapore's future challenges. However, it raises many of the existential questions that Singaporeans will have to grapple with as they try to find their way in this new Asian century. ….(The) biggest gift I got from my training in (Western) philosophy was that the most important part of learning was not in finding the right answers. It was in finding the right questions. A deep questioning mind is an essential requirement for any Singaporean as we try to manage the unavoidable schizophrenia in our soul between our Western and Eastern identities. Raising and answering questions may seem troublesome. Yet, the one key point that both Eastern and Western philosophies agree on is that a life spent in deep reflection is the most satisfying life to have. And we Singaporeans are blessed with many big existential questions to answer."*

After graduation, you went into diplomacy and had postings to countries like Cambodia, Malaysia and USA where you were based in Washington and New York. Can you give us a glimpse of your postings to different cities?

Well, I think each posting was very different. When I was in Phnom Penh from 1973 to 1974, the city was at war. It was shelled every day and I recall bombs falling near my house and shrapnel coming in through the glass. So

I experienced living in war conditions in a real way. As someone in the mid 20s, I learnt about the brutality and dangers of war in a very direct fashion, with dead bodies on the streets after each shelling.

As for Malaysia, I was there in the 1970s. The wounds of the divorce between Malaysia and Singapore in 1965 were still very alive. So there was a reasonable degree of hostility towards Singapore diplomats in Kuala Lumpur then. But at the same time, at a personal level, the Malaysians could not have been nicer. They were very warm and friendly and I actually made lifelong friendships with many of the Malaysian diplomats I met. So I know for a fact that, despite political differences, you can make deep personal friendships.

My next posting was in Washington DC from 1982 to 1984. It was of course the Rome of the 20th century. And, as you know, all roads lead to Rome. Everybody wanted a piece of the action in Washington, it being the capital of the world's most powerful country. Overall being based there was a very powerful learning experience for me to understand how great powers operated.

Next I went to New York – from 1984 to 1989 and then from 1998 to 2004. I was ambassador to the United Nations twice but the two stints were vastly different. The first one was during the Cold War and the UN Security Council was dead. Nothing was happening. All the action was in the UN General Assembly where we had great debates which I enjoyed participating in – especially debates related to the Vietnamese occupation of Cambodia. By the time I had my second stint, the Cold War was over. We were living in a unipolar world of American power and the General Assembly was dead. What was alive was the UN Security Council. Therefore it was a very different United Nations. This taught me how international relations can change every decade, for instance, and nothing stands still.

Specifically, can I hear more about how exposure to diverse cities, for instance, has cultivated in you a curious mind?

Well, I would say the wonderful thing about living in different cities is that each city has its own character and identity. So it's a joy to discover the identity of each city. For example, I remember one time I was taking a taxi in New York. My driver happened to be a migrant from Sweden. When he heard that I studied Philosophy in Singapore, we had a very deep and intense discussion of Western philosophy. That to me was a great educational experience.

Similarly there was another taxi driver I met in New York who wasn't wealthy but a lot of his earnings went to a school in India which was educating a few hundred young girls. I remember my youngest son – who was between 10 and 12 years old then – being very moved by the story. He insisted that I must tip this driver well. So whether it is London, Paris, Tokyo or any other city, one soon learns that each city has its unique cultural organism and it's a joy to actually discover the nature of that cultural organism.

On a softer note and out of curiosity, are there some cities that you are particularly drawn to for whatever reasons?

I would say that my two favourite cities in the world are Singapore obviously and New York. They are places I have lived in long enough such that I can get underneath the skin of each city. So when I go back to New York, I feel like a native. I can go around in Manhattan with ease because of familiarity. I know how to be careful and how to avoid being mugged. These are things you learn about a place only after you have lived there long enough.

Interestingly, you mentioned Singapore. Can we hear a little bit more?

Well, I think Singapore is frankly one of the most dazzling cities in the world because it's the only global city where you have four major civilizations interacting in a dynamic way on a daily basis. You have Chinese civilization, Indian civilization, Islamic civilization and Western civilization – all under one roof. And I don't know of any other city in the world where you have these four civilizations alive – functioning and doing well and living in peace with each other. That's a unique Singapore attribute. Which is why I say that Singapore will become the capital of the Asian century. It's where all the three major civilization streams of Asia – Chinese, Indian and Islamic – come through. That's why we are really a special city and yet this reality is sometimes under appreciated.

This assessment from someone who has been well exposed globally is instructive because Singaporeans often can't wait to go far away to explore the world. On a personal note, how do you rediscover Singapore, especially during this pandemic when we are not able to travel much?

One of the things I'm very proud of is that during the height of the pandemic, I ran or walked a lot. I covered an average of 11 kilometers a day in 2021 – meaning about 4000 kilometers a year, going by my Fitbit's record. Walking is one of the best ways to discover a city. I walk a lot in the parks naturally but sometimes also in other places. For example, at the height of the pandemic when we couldn't go and eat in restaurants, I would try to look for *char kway teow* in places like East Coast Road or Joo Chiat Road. If you are interested in food, it is very hard to find another place that has as much variety as what Singapore offers.

You were twice Singapore's Ambassador to the UN and served as President of the UN Security Council. These were global roles which called for application of a range of complex skills. With regard to communication and negotiation in particular, can you give us a glimpse of the challenges?

The most powerful lesson I learned after years as Singapore's ambassador to the UN is that when you're a diplomat from a small country, you don't have power on your side and I have said power is the most important factor in international relations. So I will tell the staff of the Singapore embassy that we walk into the UN with only three weapons – reason, logic and charm. You have to deploy these weapons to get people to listen to you. I was actually very heartened that even though we were in the Security Council representing a very small country, the speeches made by our delegates were listened to very carefully because people knew that we put a lot of effort into writing reasonable and thoughtful speeches.

One of the biggest compliments we got was when the deputy Russian ambassador once told us how he advised his delegates to look at our speeches as a guide whenever they wanted to discuss an issue in the UN Security Council. That meant a lot. Afterall, Russia is one of the most powerful countries in the world and Singapore is one of the least powerful countries in the world. I guess we could get our speeches listened to because we were reasonable, logical and analytical. The power of reasoning and logic becomes that much more compelling in a setting like the UN where speeches are translated into different languages. If a speech is reasonable and logical, it is easier to translate.

You talk about the three attributes or what you term "the three weapons" – reason, logic and charm. Do you recall a satisfying experience when reason, logic or charm came in helpful in a difficult situation – like when there was negotiation over a particular matter?

During the Cold War in the 1980s, Singapore was more sympathetic to the United States. We were not anti-Soviet Union but it had supported the Vietnamese invasion of Cambodia and invaded Afghanistan. Singapore was very critical of these moves, so we would debate them in the UN. One day, the Cuban Ambassador, speaking as a small state which was close to the Soviet Union, defended the Russian invasion of Afghanistan. I used logic to show how every statement would have a universal dimension and how he was in fact also supporting the argument that it would be reasonable or justifiable for the United States to invade Cuba.

Next, let's hear more about your transition to academia. At the Lee Kuan Yew School of Public Policy in NUS, you were Dean from 2004 to 2017 and Professor in the Practice of Public Policy from 2006 to 2019. How was the transition from diplomacy to academia like for you?

I was fortunate. I already had half a foot in academia even before I joined the university. As a diplomat, I was already writing. (***Editor's Note:*** *Professor Mahbubani was the first diplomat from Singapore to publish an article in the* *magazine Foreign Affairs in 1983.*) Some 21 years before I became Dean at the Lee Kuan Yew School of Public Policy at the National University of Singapore, I had already published articles.

In the 1990s, I spent a year doing a sabbatical in Harvard University. That year, I published several articles so I already had an interest in academia. Wherever I was posted, I would make it a point to be plugged into the intellectual community – whether I was in Kuala Lumpur, Washington or New York. So for me the transition from diplomacy to academia wasn't difficult. I recall former Deputy Prime Minister Dr Tony Tan reminding me to publish as Dean of the Lee Kuan Yew School of Public Policy when we had lunch in New York. I think he expected me to publish one book as Dean. I am glad I ended up with six or seven books and he was very surprised.

So in your case there wasn't a stark divide because you were already engaged with the academic community. Let's next talk a little bit about your role as an intellectual and writer. In your global communication, as a speaker and a writer, what are some of your guiding principles? *(Editor's Note: In April 2019, Professor Mahbubani was elected as an honorary international member to the American Academy of Arts and Sciences which has honoured distinguished thinkers, including several of America's founding fathers, since 1780. He has spoken in many corners of the world and published in globally renowned journals and newspapers like Foreign Affairs, Foreign Policy, New York Times and Financial Times.)*

I think the first principle is don't be boring. And don't be super cautious. When I started writing as a civil servant, I was told to be careful so as to avoid getting into trouble or losing my job. In Singapore, we have a culture where people tend to be super cautious. For me, I have always wanted to write clearly and boldly.

I've always emphasized that I learned at the feet of three great masters – Lee Kuan Yew, Goh Keng Swee and S. Rajaratnam (the founding fathers of modern Singapore). All three were brilliant writers – very bold, direct and blunt. They never waffled or beat about the bush. To me, that's the way to engage people and get their attention – get to the point, be direct and state your point clearly and boldly. I think if I had not spent time talking to these three leaders and watching them, I would never have been able to write the way I do now.

Editor's Note: *For a sense of how Professor Mahbubani applies some of the writing principles he talks about above, consider this extract from a piece he wrote for Newsweek Opinion in August 2021.*

"China has been around for 5,000 years. The United States has been around for 250 years. And it's not surprising that a juvenile like the United States would have difficulty dealing with a wiser, older civilization. So the troubles that the United States is having in dealing with China are perfectly understandable. What the United States doesn't understand is the longer arc of human history. There's a British historian called Angus Maddison who pointed out that if you look at the history of the world over the past 2,000 years, the two largest economies of the world have always been those of China and India. It's only in the last 200 years that the West took off, Europe in the 19th century and North America in the 20th century. The past 200 years of world history have been a major historical aberration and all aberrations come to a natural end. It's perfectly natural to see the West retreat to its normal share of global power. And there are some things in the longer arc of human history that cannot be stopped. So the return of China, and subsequently India, are perfectly natural developments. Of course it's perfectly natural for the United States, which has got used to being number one since they replaced the British in 1819, to feel a sense of entitlement, that they should always be number one in the world. What the United States lacks in dealing with China is a comprehensive long-term strategy, which is what you need to deal with one of the oldest civilizations on planet earth. This insight actually was given to me by Henry Kissinger."

Political leaders aside, I'm sure you would also have some intellectual giants that you were drawn to, people who might have influenced you in your writing?

I think what I found in my year in Harvard was this – the greatest people are those who would disagree with your ideas and yet listen to them with respect. I'll give you an example. One of the most famous writers that Harvard University has produced is the late Professor Samuel Huntington – famous for his "clash of civilizations" theory. His worldview was very different from mine but he would always listen intently to me. I was very impressed by that. Then of course there is Larry Summers who has always been very generous with his time and thoughts. Other distinguished professors whose names come to mind include Ezra Vogel, who has passed away, and Joseph Nye. That is one of the strengths of the great American universities. Even people who disagree with you will listen to you.

I want to move on to the idea of international collaboration and why it matters. You have a distinct personal voice. Yet you have also co-authored articles with distinguished global thought leaders like Kofi Annan, Klaus Schwab and Larry Summers. Why is international collaboration important for you as a thinker and writer?

Even in the world of ideas, branding is important. So if you have a good brand, people will listen to your ideas. I think Lee Kuan Yew, for instance, had a very good brand intellectually and people around the world would listen to him for his ideas. People like Kofi Annan, Klaus Schwab and Larry Summers are highly respected globally. So it is an honour for me to co-author with them. Beyond recognition and prestige, what matters most is a greater diversity of voices and wider reach in terms of more people being introduced to what you have to share.

Putting these global thought leaders as a group, will you, having worked with them, share with us your general impressions of them?

I think Kofi Annan was probably one of the most successful in his role as UN Secretary General. He was a very humble person yet he was quite shrewd in his handling of the great powers like the United States, Russia and China.

Klaus Schwab has a remarkable accomplishment because the World Economic Forum, which he started as a small scale event, is by far the most successful international gathering of its kind today. To keep a global forum like this going, you need not only vision but also energy and drive – and he has been indefatigable in setting the gold standard.

Larry Summers is, I would say, one of the brainiest persons. He is easily one of the hardest persons to argue with because his brain has got tremendous capacity. Not unexpectedly, he can be very forceful in his argument but he would respect you for arguing back. So I have always felt that when you engage him, it is like trying to push back a 10-tonne truck. Yet he will listen to you and when he thinks you have a good point, you will say "You're right and I am wrong."

Listening to your assessment of some of these global personalities, I can't resist asking: What about some Asian intellectual giants that have impressed you?

I consider Amartya Sen to be one of the greatest Asian thinkers. He is a great global public intellectual and his book *The Argumentative Indian* is brilliantly written. Former Indian Prime Minister Manmohan Singh – thoughtful and intellectual – will also be rated right up there.

And of course I have already mentioned the three figures whose influence I appreciate – Lee Kuan Yew, Goh Keng Swee and S. Rajaratnam. There are others but if I may just add one more name, it will be Professor Wang Gungwu, the great historian. To me, he is a real treasure and we're fortunate to have him in Singapore.

As a prolific author, you have published thought-provoking books which provide an Asian perspective for a range of issues. Such books include *Can Asians Think?*, *The New Asian Hemisphere*, *The Great Convergence*, *Can Singapore Survive?*, *Has the West Lost It?* and *Has China Won?* Can you share with us how you see your role as an author?

The best test of any idea is the market test. When books are published, it is quite normal for them to go out of print after two or three years. They are born and many die with no reprint. They just disappear into the tombs of history. So it is satisfying that my first book – a collection of essays entitled *Can Asians Think?* which came out in 1998 – is still alive and well after 24 years. There have been four different editions. Starting off as a thin paperback edition, it now has a thick hardcover edition. For me, if a book can still be on sale after 24 years, it shows that the ideas remain valid. Yes, it is very heartening when books carry on and have a long shelf life.

I should also mention my recent book *The Asian 21st Century* which is an open access book. You can download it for free from Springer. I am very heartened by the public's response. (**Editor's Note:** *In two weeks, it had over 100,000 downloads. After some three months, there were 1.4 million downloads.*) I'm happy because, to me, it's not the money you make from books that's important. It is whether or not your ideas travel. It's satisfying to know that many of my books have been translated into different languages – not only usual ones like French, German, Dutch and Portuguese but also Arabic, Japanese and Bahasa Indonesia.

If you look at all my books, each one tries to convey one or two big ideas. *The Great Convergence*, for instance, is about global governance: What is wrong with our current system of global governance? Why was it a mistake for the United States to weaken institutions like the United Nations? The book raises the key question: Has the West lost its way at the end of the Cold War? In essence, each book should have one big idea, with details to support it. There's no point writing a book if it doesn't have one big central idea. (**Editor's Note:** *The Great Convergence was ranked by Financial Times' Martin Wolf as one of the best books of 2013 when it came out.*)

Apart from the focus on one central idea each time, would it be right to say that, in a way, you are also positioning yourself as an Asian voice?

I am proud to be regarded as an Asian voice, especially because Asia is very large and diverse. Asia is by far the largest and most diverse continent on Planet Earth. There are 4 billion people in Asia, so more than half the world's population is Asian. To write about Asia, you must have some understanding of Indian civilization, Chinese civilization, Southeast Asian civilizations and cultures, and so on and so forth. So it's not easy. In contrast, Western culture and civilization can be said to be much more homogeneous. To be an Asian voice carries a big responsibility because you have to be able to speak about many different parts of Asia, which are actually very different from each other.

I think there is, in essence, the issue of credibility and ethos. You are also very familiar with the West and have lived in Western cities. How important do you think one's global exposure is before one can claim to be speaking on behalf of Asia to some extent at least?

The advantage of having spent time in the West is that I've learned to understand how the Western intellectuals argue and how the power of reasoning works there. So quite often I use Western methods of reasoning to show how Western understanding of Asia is flawed. That helps. I guess that in part explains the interest in a book like *Has China Won?* which has been translated into French, German, Portuguese and Dutch.

You have received international recognition for your works which have been described as thoughtful and provocative. My next question is this: Can you give us a sense of the beginnings of your intellectual journey – eg what was it like for you growing up as a child in terms of interests and influences?

Editor's Note: *The Foreign Policy Association Medal was awarded to Professor Mahbubani in New York in 2004 with the following opening words in the citation: "A gifted diplomat, a student of history and philosophy, a provocative* *writer and an intuitive thinker." He was also selected as one of Foreign Policy's Top Global Thinkers in 2010 and 2011 and has been described as "the muse of the Asian century." In addition, he was selected by Prospect magazine as one of the top 50 world thinkers for 2014.*

I actually came from a relatively poor family. At the age of six, I was put in a special feeding program in school as I was technically undernourished and we were on welfare. We had debt collectors coming to our home. So mine was the typical Third World childhood. But what saved me was that the Joo Chiat Public Library was located less than a mile from my house. I don't know how but at the age of maybe eight, nine or 10, I discovered this library. My parents didn't go to university and never encouraged me to read. We didn't have books in our house of course as we didn't even have enough money for food. Yet I fell in love with books. I would borrow three or four books a week from the library and bring them home and read. If I hadn't gone to the library as a child, I would never be where I am today.

Can you recall some books or at least topics that you were fascinated with?

I would read everything, covering a whole range of writers. For fiction, I went for authors like Leo Tolstoy and Fyodor Dostoyevsky. I would also read nonfiction and was drawn to Aldous Huxley, for instance. I was very lucky that I had a childhood friend from the age of six – Jeffrey Sng who would later become my co-author for the book, *The ASEAN Miracle: A Catalyst for Peace*. He and I used to go together to the Joo Chiat Public Library. We both loved books and that was how we ended up in university.

In terms of cultivating a curious mind, we know the value of global exposure, whether through traveling or living overseas. So finally Professor Mahbubani, what's your advice for our young people today?

When I was young, all we aspired to as young people was to go to London, New York, Paris or one of the other great Western cities. Looking back at my early life, my love for these Western cities was understandable. I spent the first 15 years of my life, from 1948 to 1963, in a British colony. In a way, my generation was politically and mentally colonised. Growing up, we had the "West is best" mindset. I once had a conversation with a primary school classmate who said he would like to go to London because its streets were paved with gold.

But I think it's important for the young today to understand that the centre of gravity of the world's economy has now shifted to East Asia. It's no more in Europe. It's no more in America. So if I were a young Singaporean today, I should know that the most interesting part of Planet Earth is Southeast Asia. Among the 650 million people in this region, you have so many diverse groups – Muslims, Christians, Buddhists, Taoists, Confucianists etc. So Southeast Asia is by far the most diverse and most interesting corner on Planet Earth and we are now blessed to be living in this region.

Indeed, this is the best place to watch the Asian century unfold. It is the only place on Planet Earth that has experienced the impact of four major world civilisations: Indian, Chinese, Muslim and Western. Hence, as the world moves on from a mono-civilisational world dominated by the West to a multi-civilisational world of many thriving civilisations, we need to look for a multi-civilisational laboratory that will reveal what a multi-civilisational world will look like. There is only one multi-civilisational laboratory in the world: South-east Asia.

To the young, I will say this: To prepare for the future, make sure you understand at least one or two other Southeast Asian countries as well as you understand yours. That will give you a huge competitive advantage. It's your choice which country. For me, I love Indonesia, for example. I think it is a fascinating country. But it could be Thailand, Vietnam or the Philippines too. As a child, I used to believe that I was unfortunate in being born on the wrong side of the world. Now, at my age, I realise there is no better place in the world to be than in South-east Asia.

Editor's Note: *To appreciate Professor Mahbubani's in-depth understanding and love of Southeast Asia, we offer here an extract from a piece he penned for The Straits Times in April 2017.*

"South-east Asia [with the four waves of history that have swept through it over the past 2,000 years] is the go-to place to understand the new 21st century world…...Some may think that this history is dead and buried. Indeed, the first dominant wave to hit South-east Asia, the Indian wave, lasted a thousand years and petered out about a thousand years ago. When the Indian rulers became preoccupied with the overland invasions from the north-west, they lost their maritime connections with South-east Asia. However, the Indian wave remains deeply embedded in the South-east Asian psyche. President Suharto was a Muslim ruling the world's most populous Muslim-majority country, Indonesia. Yet, when he wanted to make a statement on how well Indonesia was progressing, he chose to erect an enormous statue of the Mahabharata warrior, Arjuna, in the heart of Jakarta in 1987. How did a civilisational wave that disappeared a thousand years ago continue to exercise a magical influence on Indonesian minds? Thailand is a deeply Buddhist country. It reveres its king. However, if you observe Thai court rituals closely, you will notice that many are conducted by Hindu Brahmin priests. One great mystery of South-east Asian history is that, despite the fact that China is geographically closer, nine out of the 10 South-east Asian societies have an Indian cultural sub-structure rather than a Chinese one…...Even more remarkably, the Indianised kingdoms of South-east Asia used to pay tribute to China, not to India. In short, South-east Asia has had close links with China and India for thousands of years……The big question for the 21st century is whether South-east Asia will resume its traditional role of being a bridge between Chinese and Indian civilisations. And will it take on a new historical role of becoming a bridge between Islam and the West?"

IF I WERE A YOUNG SINGAPOREAN

"So if I were a young Singaporean today, I should know that the most interesting part of Planet Earth is Southeast Asia. Among the 650 million people in this region, you have so many diverse groups – Muslims, Christians, Buddhists, Taoists, Confucianists etc. So Southeast Asia is by far the most diverse and most interesting corner on Planet Earth and we are now blessed to be living in this region. Indeed, this is the best place to watch the Asian century unfold. It is the only place on planet earth that has experienced the impact of four major world civilisations: Indian, Chinese, Muslim and Western. Hence, as the world moves on from a mono-civilisational world dominated by the West to a multi-civilisational world of

Picture courtesy of Kishore Mahbubani

many thriving civilisations, we need to look for a multi-civilisational laboratory that will reveal what a multi- civilisational world will look like. There is only one multi-civilisational laboratory in the world: South-east Asia. To the young, I will say this: To prepare well for the future, make sure you understand at least one or two other Southeast Asian countries as well as you understand yours. That will give you a huge competitive advantage. It's your choice which country. For me, I love Indonesia, for example. I think it is a fascinating country. But it could be Thailand, Vietnam or the Philippines too. As a child, I used to believe that I was unfortunate in being born on the wrong side of the world. Now, at my age, I realise there is no better place in the world to be than in South-east Asia."

—Kishore Mahbubani

SEEING, HEARING, FEELING, SENSING

"Suddenly you're not just seeing but hearing, feeling, sensing Washington, Panama, South Africa, as they look today but also as they may seem a hundred years from now. How many writers have been able to take a place and weave a thousand details and feelings and moments into a single near-definitive portrait, which almost seems to stand outside of time? Exactly one: Jan Morris. For 60 years she's been blending acute insights and warm intuitions into uniquely fluent, imperturbable and evocative descriptions. She's not so much traveller as historian, witness, master of classical English prose and impressionist all at once. You can find these graces in all of her books, of course, but for me the long-form essays in Destinations: Essays from Rolling Stone *offer the best (biggest) space in which her eloquence, shrewdness and wisdom can take flight. Read her on Los Angeles, Manhattan or New Delhi and you'll never want to read anyone else on those places again."*

PICO IYER ON *DESTINATIONS* BY JAN MORRIS

Source: The Guardian

BLUE OCEAN

Picture courtesy of Koh Buck Song

*"Experimenting with haiga is one realisation of the 'blue ocean' approach
I apply to life – to keep looking for new fields of endeavour in which
pioneering work is possible…..With haiga, I was curious to see what I could
make of this art form that is very rarely practised, even though man has
been creating art since his caveman rock painting days. Across the art world,
across time, it's very seldom to have visual images and words on the same
canvas – only in places like ancient Egyptian hieroglyphics, or traditional
Chinese shan shui (山水) painting. It's often said that 'a picture paints a
thousand words', but with haiga, I want to flip that around and say: 'A word
prompts a thousand mental pictures'. Haiga is a blue ocean also because it
is an art form with higher barriers to entry – both for the poet-artist's skills
and also for audience appreciation."*

—Koh Buck Song

CHAPTER 2

Think Global, Stay Global

Koh Buck Song
Poet, Author & Brand Adviser

Pictures courtesy of Koh Buck Song

Buck Song, I'm struggling with how to begin this interview, given the breadth and depth of your career. So let me take the easy way out for a start by going topical and look at *Around The World In 68 Days* – your 2021 book which has been described as "a travelogue with a big difference." So what is the "big difference" between your book *Around The World In 68 Days* and other travel books?

The "big difference" is in the way that this travelogue is unconventional – how it's not about where to go, or what to see. Instead, it seeks to distil the nation brand essence – the quintessential attributes – of each of the 13 countries and territories visited on this 68-day trip. Every chapter is an exploration of key ideas that are special to each place, and how these perceptions help elucidate where that place stands in relation to its international reputation. Also, each chapter opens with an artwork of "haiga" – a modern interpretation of a 16th-century art form in Japan – in which a haiku and an ink sketch capture images that could serve as a national metaphor for that place.

Here, I am applying perspectives developed from my practice in place branding since 2010, when I started writing the first edition of my book *Brand Singapore*. Since then, whenever I come across another country – whether on my travels, or just in online research – I'm invariably intrigued, and curious, to learn more about how heritage, culture and other factors have moulded how a place is perceived by the rest of the world, and what is happening now, or could happen, to shape its brand further in future.

This trip was completed in 2018, but because the book's publication was delayed by the pandemic, I had the chance to edit and re-edit the draft, starting from page one, with a deeper "Covid-19 sense" of a world in which travel and everything else had been totally disrupted. This was when I decided to infuse the whole text with the guiding philosophy of "ichigo ichie" ("one time, one moment"), the Japanese concept of cherishing life's worthwhile moments because any encounter is, in some way, a once-in-a-lifetime experience. One of my hopes for this book is to inspire readers to see the world anew with a more intense feel for "ichigo ichie".

Editor's Note: *For a better sense of the journey undertaken by Koh and its larger significance, here are extracts from the book's Prologue.*

"*Our itinerary covered thirteen territories in this order: United Arab Emirates, Oman, Madagascar, Kenya, Spain, Colombia, Costa Rica, Cuba, Panama, Mexico, Guatemala, Japan and Taiwan. In this journey, a few key aspects coalesced: the wonder of travel in general, and in particular, that special category of a continuous trip around the globe; the magic of each moment of discovery and insight on the road; and the joy of glimpsing the essence of a range of societies that are so different from each other and yet have so much in common.....Starting in Singapore, the route took in terrain of varied contrasts, from skyscrapers shooting out of barren, empty desert in the UAE to the lush 'botanical Galapagos' of Madagascar, replete with unique plants and wildlife. Despite human intervention and damage, the endless marvels of nature abound everywhere, from the 'big five' animals of Kenya to the smallest creatures of Costa Rica.*"

"*In the massive gallery of this globe, brushstrokes of the human story have been painted on many, many canvases. Each trip is like a peek into a kaleidoscope, and travel can make possible only brief glances through each lens. Narratives of how man has always striven to survive and thrive vary according to vastly different environments. Colonialism's legacy can be examined everywhere, from a former imperial power like Spain, still a formidable cultural force, to its former colonies such as Colombia and Guatemala, still recovering from the political, economic and cultural invasions and impositions of eras past, or, in the case of Cuba, still navigating a way out of isolation towards some semblance of regional and global connection.*"

"*Just as fascinating are the case studies of the enduring legacies of ancient civilizations, from the Maya and Aztecs in Mexico to the Ryukyu people in Japan. And always intriguing is the condition of small states seeking their place on the world stage, whether, as in Oman, finessing a delicate balance between preserving tradition and pursuing modernity; or, as in Panama, being buffeted literally by the waves from two oceans and figuratively from global competition; or, as in Taiwan, yearning to emerge from the shadows of its past. Covid-19 has called a timeout on all these human struggles. But the indomitable human spirit will surely rise again, and resume these yearnings for survival, success and support from other nations."*

It has been said that, in a time of a global pandemic, the book is also "a type of memoir, a tribute to travel, of a pre-Covid-19 world", "a 68-day extravaganza of ichigo ichie, the Japanese concept of cherishing every worthwhile moment". I, for one, was first drawn to the book by the notion of "ichigo ichie" and gather it is fitting that you, a brand expert, have come out with a catchy hook for the readers. There must be some truth to that from the practical perspective of publicity but, given your background, there is more depth in this as well, I presume. Can you provide both sides of the coin, so to speak?

Yes, the "ichigo ichie" aspect of this book appears to have resonated most with audiences thus far. I'm sure the way that we have all come to see the world, and ourselves, differently under social isolation and lockdown has something to do with this. What you call "the other side of the coin" with "ichigo ichie" in this book is truly something I feel deeply, that I realise I had tried to apply in my life previously. And now, I believe I have become even better able to articulate this concept with this spiritual reference, that is so simple and yet so profound.

Editor's Note: *In his book, Koh develops the idea of "ichigo ichie" further. He says: "Ichigo ichie is, in some ways, more profound than the better known phrase carpe diem (Latin for 'pluck' or 'seize' the day'), attributed to the ancient Roman poet Horace, meaning to enjoy the pleasures of the moment while minimizing concerns for the future. By contrast, ichigo ichie can be said to advise quite the opposite – to be more fully aware of the future so as to appreciate the present even better. If ichigo ichie should already transform everyday life, then its power becomes that much stronger when one is travelling. The greatest motivation, and reward, for those who love to see the world is the sense that everything one sees in a foreign country is fresh, interesting and worth remembering. Visiting* *a new place is already a treat. Going around the world takes the awareness of ichigo ichie to a whole new level."*

This sense of newness and appreciation explains the way Koh responds to the things he sees on this trip. As he puts it in his poetic language: "Within the pages of this book, there are no expert analyses, merely momentary glimpses into thirteen societies, in a time before Covid-19, by someone who simply had the good fortune to visit these places, to have an opportunity to feel their essence, if only for a while, through all the five senses: To see the vastness and variety of the wilderness, from a cheeky cloud dancing on the edge of a mountain peak to the tiniest, hardly visible, tree frog. To hear the unbridled joy of a hummingbird's chirp and the possible jealousy in a lioness growl. To smell the spices and array of savouries in a souq, and the accumulated natural fertilizers of the savannah. To touch the outstretched reaches of humanity, from the metallic-smooth terrace balcony of the world's tallest skyscraper at sunrise to the rough, weathered stone walls of an ancient monument of sun worship. To taste the Earth's boundless nutrition and nectar, from the sashimi of southernmost islands to the juice of a baobab fruit."

OK, let's next take a look at your career, starting with the present and then moving backwards. Where you are now, you are best described as "a country brand adviser, advocate of liveable and sustainable cities, and commentator on society and public policy". Broadly, can you give us a sense of what these roles involve (eg the kind of work you do and some specific skills needed to do a good job)?

Being a country brand adviser involves advising governments, and government agencies, about aspects of building a country brand, such as which are the key brand attributes, and how these can be presented at their best, so as to resonate most powerfully with foreign audiences. Sometimes, working with a foreign government, there is also an element of fostering bilateral relations with Singapore – which means that I'm thereby also doing some good for my own country. Invariably, the work has to do with applying soft power, and much of the action today happens online. There are many areas here in which having a keen sense of curiosity is very useful, for example, understanding the psychology behind past audience reactions on social media, and predicting their future responses.

More specifically, I want to take a closer look at your role as branding adviser. Among the more than 30 books you have been involved in as author and editor, there is a series on Brand Singapore. In 2011, there was *Brand Singapore: How Nation Branding Built Asia's Leading Global City*. This was followed by *Brand Singapore: Nation Branding After Lee Kuan Yew, In A Divisive World* in 2017. Then in 2021, we had *Brand Singapore: Nation Branding In A World Disrupted By Covid-19*. Can you give us a sense of the broad thinking behind your books on country branding which may not be as familiar a concept as branding in the business context? How did you discover your niche? What was the distinctive message for each of the three titles?

I discovered this niche of country branding around 2010 when my publisher, Marshall Cavendish – who also published the book *Brand America* by the guru of nation branding, Simon Anholt – was thinking of doing a similar book for Singapore. Being asked to write this book was a classic case of "being in the right place at the right time". Working in country branding, I came to realise that everything I had done before in my career turned out to be relevant, in different ways:

- Critiquing brand Singapore as a Straits Times journalist and columnist;
- Crafting and promoting brand Singapore as head of global media relations, and later, strategic planning, at the Economic Development Board; and
- Consulting to many government agencies with the international communications consultancy Hill & Knowlton, on projects such as the global launch of Gardens by the Bay and the National Gallery.

There are two other aspects. One has to do with involvement with the arts as a poet and literary editor. These roles gave me a first-hand, ground-up appreciation of the sphere of culture. Two is related to my public service as a member of three Censorship Review Committees and many other citizen advisory panels. All this added to my understanding – behind the scenes, as it were – of how Singapore manages access to all media content. These are all ingredients of cultural soft power. Thus, I was able to offer both an independent insider-and-outsider perspective on brand Singapore, which is relatively uncommon in this field, as writers on country branding typically come from one main field, such as consultancy or academia. Since publishing *Brand Singapore*, I have had the opportunity a few times to speak on brand Singapore overseas, such as at the City Nation Place global forum in London. I've also had the chance to act as an adviser to foreign governments on building their nation brands.

The broad thinking behind this series of *Brand Singapore* books is to achieve two aims at once. The first is to offer an introduction to the field of country branding, including for those who are new to this subject. The second aim is to present Singapore as a case study of nation brand-building, with a succinct overview and analysis of the whole history of its country brand since independence. In each new edition (planned to be released roughly five years apart), the content is updated with assessments of recent developments and challenges for the mid- and longer-term future ahead.

In terms of a "distinctive message" for each edition, the 2011 first edition, *Brand Singapore: How Nation Branding Built Asia's Leading Global City*, sought to highlight the key circumstances and resources of Singapore affecting its brand. These range from innovative government initiatives to continually enhance the island's hard infrastructure (such as the "City in nature" plan to integrate nature into the urban fabric by, for example, "retrofitting" canals back into rivers with grass banks) to unique approaches to the most intangible issues (such as the public housing ethnic quota policy to help manage race relations). The book also examines the strategies and efforts, and successes and challenges, of the public, private and people sectors in enabling Singapore to establish and sustain an international reputation as a leading global city.

The second edition in 2017, *Brand Singapore: Nation Branding After Lee Kuan Yew, In A Divisive World*, refreshed the content by adding analyses of key events since 2011. These would include the SG50 anniversary of 50 years of independence and the passing of founding Prime Minister Lee Kuan Yew, as well as the backdrop of a world seeing the beginnings of game-changing trends such as deglobalisation, challenging Singapore's "global city" positioning, the focus of the book's first edition. The third edition in 2021, *Brand Singapore: Nation Branding In A World Disrupted By Covid-19*, aims to absorb the impact of the many key events since 2017, including the presidential election of 2017, the 2018 movie "Crazy Rich Asians" set in Singapore, the Bicentennial year of 2019 and the general election of 2020, as well as the initial global upheaval brought by the Covid-19 pandemic.

Apart from books, your work as brand adviser also involves talks and seminars at institutions like Harvard, MIT, Chicago University, Oxford University, Melbourne University, Fudan University and the Japan Foundation. Interestingly, there have even been opportunities in lesser-known places like Phuentsholing, Bhutan, and Tahiti, French Polynesia. Can you give us a glimpse of the work involved in terms of the global talks and seminars you have taken part in? In particular, how did doors open for locations like Phuentsholing and Tahiti, and what were the experiences there like beyond the formal work?

In Bhutan, I was invited to speak on nation branding at the Royal Institute for Governance and Strategic Studies in Phuentsholing. The King of Bhutan has a keen interest in nation branding, and someone gave him a copy of the second edition of my book on "Brand Singapore", and that led to the invitation. Bhutan already has one of the world's most recognised country brands, but, nonetheless, it wants to find new ways to expand the reach of its brand, to boost the economy and lift living standards further. It's intriguing to compare and contrast Bhutan and Singapore, as the two societies are almost polar opposites in some ways, for example, on the spectrum between tradition and modernity, or spirituality and materialism.

In Tahiti, I was invited by the Pacific Economic Cooperation Council to speak at a symposium on sustainable tourism that included speakers from the US, Australia, the Pacific islands and Taiwan. A friend of mine from the international relations circles recommended me for this. One key takeaway from this seminar is that tourism can be sustainable only if the local population is also invested in its development. Visiting Tahiti also prompted me to begin pondering the legacy of French colonialism, compared with British imperialism, which I later studied further on my 68-day trip in Madagascar, another French territory.

Since February 2014, you have served as adjunct editor for The Centre for Liveable Cities – the research centre and think-tank under the Ministry of National Development which seeks to "distil, create and share knowledge on liveable and sustainable cities". Among other things, your work involves editing books and reports related to major events such as the World Cities Summit Mayors Forum and Young Leaders Symposium. You have also conducted video interviews with Singapore's Prime Minister Lee Hsien Loong and London Mayor Boris Johnson (now British Prime Minister). Generally, what is your approach towards written communication as opposed to spoken communication, both of which are rather different, as we well know?

Written and spoken communication are different mainly in delivery mode, duration and demand for off-the-cuff responses. But in terms of preparation, the approaches for both are really quite the same. First is the need to do adequate research, which requires double-checking not only data, but also being curious enough to re-examine the sometimes unintended, and possibly pejorative, connotations of even commonly-used words. Next is the need for a neat, easy-to-understand conceptual framework to organise the points to be communicated. Finally, sequence and phrase everything well so that the words are clear and succinct, and also engaging as well. One can also make reference to points of interest to target audiences so as to resonate with, and even inspire, them.

Next, let's explore an area you have ventured into which I am particularly intrigued by. I am referring to your role as a haiga-poet artist. I understand you discovered the form in 2015 while you were reading up on Japan ahead of a trip there at the invitation of the Japan Foundation. **Regarding how you became a haiga-poet artist, there is clearly a story on curiosity. Can you share more?**

Editor's Note: Buck Song has been practising and promoting haiga, a 16th-century Japanese art form combining poetry and visual art, since 2016. He has had exhibitions, starting with the first one "Six Views Of Japan And Singapore" at the Esplanade in 2016 where he captured images from the two countries in simple ink sketches "accompanied by haiku that range from the introspective to the humorous". There was also an exhibition held in Vientiane, Laos, in 2017 to commemorate the 50th anniversary of ASEAN.

Experimenting with haiga is one realisation of the "blue ocean" approach I apply to life – to keep looking for new fields of endeavour in which pioneering work is possible. It's a way of thinking that I try to apply every day, since first coming across the blue ocean strategy when I was working at the Economic Development Board, where I overheard entrepreneurs constantly being exhorted to seek new opportunities. "Blue ocean" refers to a marketing theory by INSEAD professors W. Chan Kim and Renée Mauborgne, on how to avoid "red ocean" areas where there are many "sharks" already feeding, hence the "blood staining the water". For me, working in country branding is one such blue ocean space, as there are still surprisingly few practitioners around the world, let alone in Singapore.

With haiga, I was curious to see what I could make of this art form that is very rarely practised, even though man has been creating art since his caveman rock painting days. Across the art world, across time, it's very seldom to have visual images and words on the same canvas – only in places like ancient Egyptian hieroglyphics, or traditional Chinese *shan shui* (山水) painting. It's often said that "a picture paints a thousand words", but with haiga, I want to flip that around and say: "A word prompts a thousand mental pictures".

Haiga is a blue ocean also because it is an art form with higher barriers to entry – both for the poet-artist's skills and also for audience appreciation. I have modernised the haiku poem with a few innovations – adding a title, and rhyme in the first and third lines. I've also added a dimension of country branding to my practice of haiga – each haiga seeks to capture the brand essence of that place, as for all 13 countries featured in my book *Around the World in 68 Days*. There's an element of building people-to-people relations through the cultural exchange that art enables too. For my ASEAN 50th anniversary exhibitions, in each of the haigas for all 10 Southeast Asian nations, I used a word from that country's language. For Singapore, the word is in the title: Marina Bay *hoseh* ("everything's good" in Singlish).

When you discovered haiga, which involves poetry and visual arts, you were already an established poet but the other medium was new to you though you might have been interested in it. Through your initiation into haiga, can you give us a glimpse of what it was like picking up something new? From this case of picking up haiga and other personal experiences, what would be your wider message for the young in this age of constant learning and skills upgrading?

Editor's Note: By other personal experiences, we refer to, for instance, Koh's transition from journalism to global media relations to communications consultancy as well as his move to study Public Administration at Harvard University following his pursuit of English Literature at Cambridge.

I've had an interest in drawing and sketching since childhood when I would draw Spider-Man and other comic book characters in jotter books for my schoolmates. So trying my hand at haiga was applying something I could already do, but in a way that works well within the boundaries of that art form, where the techniques and other demands are different from what is required to "compete" in the "red ocean" of conventional visual art forms. From this, one wider message for the young would be to keep on learning and trying new skills, and to start with something you're reasonably good at, at first, and then build from there. If you can also find a blue ocean space to try this out, that would be a bonus.

Still on haiga, you have also said this: "… (it) is an art form particularly conducive to our times, in this cyber age of short attention spans, in which concise, meaningful words and a striking visual element – on Facebook, for example – are what catches people's attention best. Haiga can be savoured and shared, complete on one smartphone screen." More broadly, you have also talked about "blue ocean" spaces for people to discover and explore. Coming from you, such themes – like moving with the times and being open to new areas – are not surprising, given the arc of your own career which has been generally characterised by constant change. Broadly, when you look back at your career, what has been some of your guiding principles, focusing on those that will resonate with the young who face unique challenges today?

One guiding principle I've had is to believe in myself, and to focus on doing something that has impact and is enduring. This is why I feel very grateful that I have writing skills that enable me to earn income from writing and editing, which have practically no retirement age. Books are a special way of leaving a legacy. Any book published will have copies kept safe in the Lee Kong Chian Reference Library at the National Library, possibly forever, unless, say, an asteroid destroys the Earth. Any digital resource, however, would be totally useless anyway unless there is electricity, wi-fi and you have a compatible device.

One approach that became even clearer to me more recently is to remind myself to expand "the universe of curiosity" and look beyond Singapore to the world. Often, forces at home can easily stunt your aspirations – like someone saying Singapore is too small for your idea to work, or that someone else might not like what you're doing, or people who would only praise those who have already arrived, like winners of international prizes or those already endorsed by someone powerful. If someone here doesn't support what you're doing, just move on; there is a potential audience of 8 billion out there.

More traditionally, you were a columnist and political and arts journalist with The Straits Times, and head of global media relations and strategic planning at Singapore's Economic Development Board. You were also head of public affairs (Southeast Asia) with the communications consultancy Hill & Knowlton – a role which involved advising the Singapore government on various aspects of urban development, including the global launch of Gardens by the Bay and the National Gallery Singapore. Broadly, what skills would be most valued in your various communication roles? Having done well in your corporate jobs, what was the impetus for you to strike out on your own?

Beyond the essential skills involved in good writing and communication, there is also the understanding of how the media works, and how to present content in ways that fit the varied audience segments. Once again, having curiosity and loads of empathy would certainly help. One main impetus to strike out on my own in my career was that I became curious to see if I could have a "portfolio career". This means not having just a single employer but investing in a self-managed working mode with multiple streams of income from part-time work or projects in a few fields. For me, these areas have included writing, editing, video interviews, and consulting in country branding, organisational branding, leadership, strategic communications and corporate social responsibility.

Membership – in institutions, for instance – brings both privileges and restrictions. In your case, on balance, what has kept you on the side of personal enterprise? With respect to traits like creativity and curiosity, how has being on your own been a boost (which I assume is indeed the case)?

For sure, if you want to stay open to fully developing your creativity and curiosity, it helps to be as free as possible from constraint and compromise. As long as you are part of an organisation, some time will be taken up by "administrative tasks" (such as keeping your bosses and colleagues informed about what you've done and are going to do) rather than doing the actual work. Also, there would be no running away from some institutional obligations. Being an independent consultant means working towards being able to choose to do only what you like to do. It also means not knowing what the next project might be, or where it might take you – for example, one writing job took me to Bangkok to cover Microsoft CEO Satya Nadella's trip to Asia; one commissioned book project took me to Tashkent, Uzbekistan.

Finally, Buck Song, one of my first interviews with you was when you published your first collection of poetry many years back. How time flies and how much things have changed! Yet interestingly, one of the poems in the collection, *A Brief History Of Toa Payoh*, includes these poignant lines: "in our History's eye/growth is so swift/rebirth also gets short shrift." Which all takes me back to *Around The World In 68 Days* where – for all your unique experiences in places like Panama, Okinawa and Madagascar – we come back to what has been termed our "shared humanity across the globe – what makes each of us unique, what we share, and how, in the end, perhaps we're all really chasing ultimately similar dreams." What have you learnt from the many cities you have been to, given the sparks that can fly when complex cities meet curious minds? Ending on a broad, sweeping note, what, to you, would be some dreams our young – guided by curiosity and all – can and should embark on?

The line you quoted from my poem "A Brief History Of Toa Payoh" alludes to the selective, self-centred perspective of the "eye" (the worldview) that we all invariably use to look at our own histories, let alone the histories of other places. This explains the "short shrift" that we tend to give to fresh knowledge – hence the value of sustaining curiosity, to comprehend new data and come up with fresh insights, so as to make fuller sense of the world.

The world is so abundantly varied, but from the many cities I've been to, there are a few aspects that resonate most with me. One centres on places that are at the nexus, the interface, of two or more worlds, such as Istanbul, between Asia and Europe, or Morocco, between Africa and Europe. Such places are always a blend of myriad influences, and it's enriching to explore how diversity transforms – and usually enhances – the character of these societies.

Another facet is the unique situation of small states, especially islands in strategic locations, or, sometimes, places surrounded by larger, troubled territories – from Singapore to Cuba or Costa Rica – that have been the focus of claims and contestations from internal and external influences throughout history. I'm always curious about how such societies cope with managing their internal challenges while opening up to engage with the world outside, such as keeping heritage and tradition afloat amidst the inexorable currents of modernity. A metaphor for this from my 68-day trip is how the turtles of Oman keep swimming against the ocean's waves, to clamber back to shore to nest every year.

As for dreams for the young, this brings us back to Brand Singapore. I believe that, for any place that aspires to be a global city, it would help if more citizens of that place try to fully grasp what country branding entails, and have ever contemplated themselves contributing towards building that brand. I would certainly love to see more young people staying curious, to think and act global, and so do their bit, however small, to add to our national brand.

Editor's Note: *For a glimpse of what the curious mind can absorb while travelling. we can do no better than offer readers extracts from Koh's book, Around The Book In 68 Days. On Oman, for instance, he notes: "In Oman, in the halls of the Royal Opera House in Muscat, we saw how ancient tradition can not only co-exist with modernity but, in fact, can also rejuvenate itself with a renewal of perspective and broadening of mindset and outlook. This develops best when inspired from the top and participated in from the bottom – and never giving up, like the turtles that clamber ashore year after year."*

Regarding Okinawa, he, noting that Japan is "a place of resilience and rebuilding," says:"Okinawa, at the edge of Southeast Asia, is an emblem of centuries of contending with foreign powers while striving to retain the core of a unique identify of cultural fusion, exemplified by its distinctive shisa lions. Shuri Castle, destroyed so many times, continues to inspire with its call for unquestioned fortitude as it re-emerges, once again, like a phoenix."

Next, writing on Cuba, he notes: "Cuba is an island of wonder, so full of rich culture and history, coveted and contested by external forces for so long. It makes for such a potent brew of so many culture clashes, especially at the interface between communism and capitalism, and between the Spanish- and English-speaking worlds. Come what may, the people's exuberance, encapsulated by the rhythms of salsa and the instinct for liberty, are an enduring triumph of the human spirit."

Finally, sharing about Madagascar, he writes:"Madagascar provided a case study of the psyche of one of the most fascinating of island nations. It was heartwarming to think about the intriguing origins of the roots of international kinships through the first ancient migrants from Southeast Asia, long before the era of French colonization. It was mind boggling to consider the courageous routes taken to seek their fortunes in flimsy canoes across treacherous oceans. Here, similar energy and enterprise are exemplified by the territory's unique wildlife, for whom the bounty of nature also holds rich rewards, from the steady stature of zebus to the daring dexterity of lemurs."

UNIVERSE OF CURIOSITY

Picture courtesy of Koh Buck Song

"One approach that became even clearer to me more recently is to remind myself to expand 'the universe of curiosity' and look beyond Singapore to the world. Often, forces at home can easily stunt your aspirations – like someone saying Singapore is too small for your idea to work, or that someone else might not like what you're doing, or people who would only praise those who have already arrived, like winners of international prizes or those already endorsed by someone powerful. If someone here doesn't support what you're doing, just move on; there is a potential audience of 8 billion out there."

—Koh Buck Song

TREASURY OF WISDOM

"I first read Arabian Sands *as a teenager. As I came to the last page, I knew that the course of my life had been altered. Thesiger had taken me on a journey through the fearful void, the Empty Quarter of the Arabian Desert, and left me desperate to embark on a great journey of my own. Sir Wilfred never intended to write the book. He told me later that he'd spent years with the Bedouin of Rub' al Khali, existing with them on their own terms. Without them, he said, 'the journeys would have been a meaningless penance'. A good travel book is a treasury of wisdom that seeps into your blood as you follow the author on their quest. And that's exactly what* Arabian Sands *achieves so well. It doesn't preach, but allows the reader to gently absorb the essence of the desert. Through fragments of description, the odd random fact, snippet of conversation, or observation, Thesiger conjured the interleaving layers of a bewitching land."*

TAHIR SHAH ON *ARABIAN SANDS* BY WILFRED THESIGER

Source: The Guardian

INTENSE IMMERSION

Picture courtesy of Debarshi Dasgupta

"I had to choose between the conventional Anglophone postgraduate educational trajectory that many Indian students take in the US or the UK and an uncertain one in France. I am glad I chose the latter. Having studied French for three years and mastered it to a respectable level in India, I wanted to live and study in France. The choice was made easier after I won a French government scholarship. In many ways, it was a risk similar to what I undertook when I agreed to spend three months at a German school on an exchange programme in my teens. I clearly have no regrets about choosing to study in France, and not in the UK or the US. I ended up learning more French in my one-year academic stint in Paris than in my three years studying the language in India. I studied Islamic Politics, focusing on Iran, and did so in French. This intense immersion in French language, together with my daily activities that were conducted in French – from shopping to chatting with my friends – embedded the language in me for life. I came back with more than just an academic degree!......(My) stay in Paris helped me familiarise myself with parts of the world that are usually overlooked by monolingual English speakers – mainly French-speaking Africa. I had classmates from north Africa and lived in a student residence that was home to scholars from many former French colonies. This opened a whole new world of literature and music for me – something I am still passionate about."

—Debarshi Dasgupta

CHAPTER 3

Inherent Diversity

Debarshi Dasgupta
India Correspondent

Pictures courtesy of Debarshi Dasgupta

Debarshi, one of the things that stands out for me is your interest in languages. You are fluent in Bengali, English, Hindi, Assamese and French and have learnt Persian at the intermediate level. Can you give us a sense of your journey in terms of learning different languages? Also, what, to you, is the deeper experience of learning a new language beyond its functional value?

Most Indians are destined to be inherently multilingual – we are a country that speaks at least 780 documented languages. One has to be extremely insensitive to this endemic linguistic diversity to become monolingual in India. I grew up speaking Bengali (my mother tongue) at home in Assam, a state where Assamese is the dominant official language. On the other hand, I studied Assamese at school in my early years and used it to converse with many of my friends, which embedded it as one of my foundation languages. I similarly acquired Hindi, which was taught to me at school and something we were exposed to through mass media, particularly television and cinema.

At home, my interest in languages was further piqued because my parents as well as my grandmother (my father's mother who lived with us) spoke Sylheti. It is a different language that, while being similar to Bengali, is not mutually intelligible. Many refer to it as a dialect of Bengali – a distinction that I fundamentally oppose. I like to believe all speech forms are languages. "A language is a dialect with an army and navy". This phrase, made popular by the sociolinguist and Yiddish scholar Max Weinreich, succinctly captures the politics of this linguistic marginalisation of dialects.

I was hooked to the idea of speech forms, languages or dialects as a window into the worldview of its speakers. This attachment was further reinforced when my school principal chose me at the age of 16 to go to a school in Germany for a three-month exchange term. I was the first student from my school to go to a non-Anglophone country for such an exchange. My stint there opened my eyes to a non-English world beyond India.

Having learnt German, I wanted to continue learning it at university but did not find a spot at Max Mueller Bhavan, which is a top centre for learning German in India. I found one at Alliance Française and began learning French the same year I started my undergraduate studies. It is something I continued for three years and later developed further during my year-long academic stint in Paris, during which I studied in French and even wrote my thesis on Indo-Iranian ties in the language.

Persian happened along the way because there were many Afghan refugees who lived in the Delhi neighbourhood I lived in back then. Many of them spoke Dari (a language similar to Farsi). I was drawn to them and their culture, as well as to the magical world of Iranian films. I regret I haven't been able to give Farsi enough time to master it as I have others because of more pressing professional concerns. I hope to change that in the next few years.

Learning a language, I feel, helps keep my intellectual faculties sharp and young, besides offering a refreshing counterbalance to my daily work. It is the same feeling one has, I guess, when he or she is picking up a new skill such as pottery or painting.

Linked to your affinity for languages is your interest in reading non-fiction, writing, photography and films. You also cite Islam and the contemporary Islamic world as an interest and have described yourself as someone who often daydreams he is "a successful morna singer in Cape Verde". Can you give us a glimpse of your exploration of your diverse interests? What would you say is the unifying, enduring theme for you and how has that shaped you both professionally and personally?

I knew I wanted to be a journalist very early in my life, probably around when I was 13 or so. My parents had a hardbound set of encyclopaedias called *Land and Peoples* and I still fondly remember how I would flick through the pages incessantly, soaking in visuals from different parts of the world and reading about diverse places, people and practices. While doing so, I imagined myself as a journalist travelling and writing about unseen places. (I still do it now but on Wikipedia where I look up remote countries and their photos!) Reading newspapers in my early teens added to that early interest for non-fiction, something I developed further along with writers such as Amitav Ghosh, William Dalrylmple, Ryszard Kapuściński, Christopher de Bellaigue and many others.

My love for writing came because I grew up in a house filled with books and with parents who encouraged reading. However, it was at school that I really honed my love for writing. I went to a residential school between the ages of 10 and 18, where I would spend eight months every year. My teachers spotted that talent in me and encouraged it profusely. I spent time reading in the school library, edited my school magazine for two years and participated with glee in several debating and elocution contests (won some of them which pushed me along).

I also picked up photography at school. I was a member of the photography club for more than four years. We learnt how to take photos using manual old-world SLR cameras and developed black and white films and prints in our school lab. It was a thrill unlike any other – seeing our work literally take shape on a paper in front of our eyes. My parents were kind enough to buy me a SLR camera in 1995 (when I was 14). That firmly set me off on a path as a photographer, something that has helped me enormously in my work as a journalist. Framing pictures using the rule of thirds – a photography skill I picked up at 13 – is something I still do.

My interest for films, I guess, are a natural extension of my identity as a journalist – someone always in pursuit of stories and willing to be hoisted from my seat and taken away on memorable journeys. Moreover, I used French and Iranian cinema as language learning tools.

The unifying, enduring theme that has shaped me greatly is, indisputably, my desire to become a journalist and my love for journalism. The desire to visit new places, learn about them and the people, pick up languages – all can be said to be related to my pursuit of this goal. The skills I have mentioned also played a role in ensuring I stayed on track to become a journalist.

My interest for Islam and the contemporary Islamic world happened because of my exposure to Afghan students and refugees around 2000, when I was at college and volunteered to teach them English. Many of them came to India, a country they could be safe in while they explored options to migrate to other countries such as those in Europe. Then 9/11 happened and an expertise on the region suddenly emerged as a potential career path too for a budding journalist such as me.

Daydreaming about Cape Verde was an attempt to introduce some levity in my bio, but it does hold a special place for me given my love for different forms of music. I keep dreaming about mastering Portuguese as well as Cape Verdean Creole, which is based on Portuguese, and enjoying Cesaria Evora's songs without referring to their English translations. It is a nice goal to have, I'd say!

Let's next look at your career path. You interned with the New Delhi edition of The Statesman while at college and then worked for Hindustan Times in Jaipur for two years, from August 2003 to August 2005, during which you reported on science, technology, environment, art and culture. Can you give us a sense of your early years at work, focusing on learning points relevant for young people? Looking back, what personal traits would you say are particularly useful for someone to thrive especially when he or she is just starting out?

I started my internship with The Statesman around 2000 when I was pursuing my undergraduate course in journalism. At that phase in my career, we were advised to take up whatever offer that came along our way. We weren't paid back then and I was compensated with only around S$10 per piece. Yet, I feel that was where I learnt the most. It is good not to have to worry about money when one is starting his or her career and instead focus more on learning. I wonder if those starting their professional careers these days have different priorities.

It was the same when I took up my first job at Hindustan Times. The salary was a pittance but the learning I imbibed during my early years there has been priceless. However, it is important to know when to pull back to avoid disillusionment. Two years into my first job, I realised I was stagnating because of the same nature of work and similar subjects that I was reporting on. This led me to apply abroad for a postgraduate course at Sciences Po in Paris.

As someone with better writing skills than others, I was often tasked with rewriting copies by my seniors as well as by others who would ask me to help them write their stories. I never used that, however, as a pretext to throw my weight around but benefited from it to build friendships with colleagues that last even until today. It is good not to be egotistic. I may have missed out on an opportunity or two but my soul feels lighter.

Then came a break from work between 2005 and 2006 during which you pursued a postgraduate degree in political science at the Institute for Political Studies in Paris. Can you share about your one year abroad both in terms of the formal education and the broader cultural experience?

I had to choose between the conventional Anglophone postgraduate educational trajectory that many Indian students take in the US or the UK and an uncertain one in France. I am glad I chose the latter. Having studied French for three years and mastered it to a respectable level in India, I wanted to live and study in France. The choice was made easier after I won a French government scholarship.

In many ways, it was a risk similar to what I undertook when I agreed to spend three months at a German school on an exchange programme in my teens. I clearly have no regrets about choosing to study in France, and not in the UK or the US. I ended up learning more French in my one-year academic stint in Paris than in my three years studying the language in India. I studied Islamic Politics, focusing on Iran, and did so in French. This intense immersion in French language, together with my daily activities that were conducted in French – from shopping to chatting with my friends – embedded the language in me for life. I came back with more than just an academic degree!

The academic programme at one of France's finest schools was also not sub par. It focused on guiding me further on my topic of research – contemporary Iran – while also introducing me to how Islam and politics have merged in different parts of the world to yield seminal political shifts such as the 1979 Islamic Revolution in Iran. As part of the curriculum, I also learnt Farsi.

I wholeheartedly recommend a stint at Sciences Po Paris to any student keen on studying abroad. I say so also because my stay in Paris helped me familiarise myself with parts of the world that are usually overlooked by monolingual English speakers – mainly French-speaking Africa. I had classmates from north Africa and lived in a student residence that was home to scholars from many former French colonies.

This opened a whole new world of literature and music for me – something I am still passionate about. How miserable I would have been without my love for various genres of African music – something I discovered and grew to love while living in France! Or without having read French-language authors such as Tahar Ben Jelloun or Ahmadou Kourouma from Africa.

Next came your seven-year stint as Special Correspondent for Outlook Magazine in New Delhi from January 2007 to March 2014. Basically you covered current affairs for the political bureau. One would imagine that the switch from a newspaper to a magazine would take storytelling to a different level. In your case, how did such a move shape your craft?

Having worked for a newspaper for two years, I began getting tired of filing multiple daily short despatches. My focus at the paper was to ensure I reported on as many breaking news stories in my beat as possible. While it seemed engrossing at the start of my career, I soon began to long for opportunities that would allow me to spend a few days working on longer stories and develop vertical knowledge in certain areas of interest. This was only going to be possible while working at a magazine, I felt. So when I returned to India to continue practising journalism, I applied to Outlook, which was and still is one of India's top news magazines.

Working for a news weekly such as Outlook gave me the time to delve into certain issues in much greater detail. I reported on science, health, environment, community affairs, tribal issues and languages – all of which were areas that I had by then developed a certain level of expertise in.

Writing for a magazine forced me to analyse specific events, which would have formed the basis for a single newspaper report, and factor them into a wider cohesive report. It involved much greater research and analytical skills, besides better writing craft. I began to think of gripping introductions rather than flat newsy ones as well as regular flourishes in the copy to keep the reader hooked. Now when I look back, it seems incredible that we had the luxury of working on a story over an entire week! This was before multimedia overwhelmed print journalism and forced us to adapt to a much more fast-paced work environment.

Editor's Note: *For a sense of the story telling that Debarshi still practises though he is now back with a newspaper, here are extracts from a piece he did in 2022 for The Straits Times as India correspondent. In this piece, he gives details of the United Nations' adoption of India's proposal to celebrate 2023 as the International Year of Millets.*

"It was about a decade ago, while shooting in rural Tamil Nadu, that actor and cardiologist Bharath Reddy first tasted millet. Until then, like most Indians reared on rice and wheat, he had little idea about this nutritious but overlooked group of grains. Someone had offered him a bowl of chunky soup made with foxtail millet and vegetables. Its 'awesome' taste ended up whetting not just his appetite, but also his curiosity. Dr Reddy, 47, began researching millets and discovered their benefits – among them the ability to slowly release their sugars into the body, in contrast with the sudden spikes seen with rice. Sold on these grains since, he has been eating them twice a day for seven years now, phasing out rice and wheat. Last year, he launched Millet Marvels, a chain of millet-based eateries in Hyderabad, to get more people to eat these grains as lifestyle diseases spiral out of control. 'Things are very, very bad and it is going to be pathetic for Indians in the next generation,' he told The Sunday Times. 'The only way you can have a healthy next lot is to change what we are eating.' Dr Reddy's endorsement of millets is part of a dramatic makeover for these grasses, cultivated for their edible seeds. Once relegated to something outmoded that our grandparents ate, millets are being plucked out of their

obscurity to be feted as a 'food of the future', thanks to their health benefits and climate-hardy nature. Millets have turned on their charm in many ways. They appear in multigrain flour mixes for wholesome rotis and feature as a healthy addition to biscuits, chips and noodles. Bakeries are making desserts with them and breweries churn out artisanal millet beer. They are also adding nutritional heft to restaurant menus across India with dishes such as millet potato fritters and millet chicken briyani. India, the world's largest producer of these cereals, now wants to replicate this globally."

With journalism as your platform, you have gone beyond day to day news to uncover issues which might otherwise lay latent. For instance, you were awarded The Laadli Media Award For Gender Sensitivity 2011/2012 for raising awareness about the secret practice of circumcision of Bohra Muslim girls. Can you say more about the stories you have done as part of investigative journalism? How crucial was the role of curiosity?

While researching on affairs related to Muslims in India as part of my regular work, I was drawn to an article in an online community portal that mentioned the practice of female circumcision in India and an online campaign to stop this. This immediately caught my attention because back then I did not know such a practice existed in India. I had heard of female genital mutilation (FGM) being practised by certain communities in Africa but was surprised it was carried out in India – and by a relatively prosperous and better educated Muslim sect. That set my reporter's instincts going.

The challenge was, however, to find Indian women who would go on record to say they had been circumcised. My report ended up being impactful because it, possibly for the first time in India, had women going on the record about being circumcised. I went through several leads, which involved talking with many women, to find some that finally worked.

I had to be curious at two levels to seal the story – first, establish that such a practice happens in India with direct quotes from victims and second, get Islamic religious scholars to tell us whether or not this practice is sanctioned by Islam. Having someone like Asghar Ali Engineer, a respected Islamic scholar, to say Islam doesn't sanction FGM added further strength to my report. My first report, which set off a much wider debate in India and built momentum for the campaign against FGM, was followed up by another report the following week that detailed the evolving campaign.

You were also awarded a 2014/2015 fellowship from the National Foundation for India, focusing on a series of 10 articles on the linguistic aspects of the Maoist conflict in India. Can you give us a glimpse of the legwork you do as an investigative reporter, including challenges faced and how you tackle them? On hindsight, what would you tell young professionals seeking advice on work involving the long, hard slough that may not yield immediate returns?

My interest in this subject arose from my reporting on linguistic affairs and marginalised communities. The left-wing rebellion, which has been going on since 1967, is one of India's deadliest conflicts. More than 10,000 lives have been lost since 2000 alone. While the conflict receives regular coverage, very little reporting has been done to explore how official cultural and linguistic marginalisation of communities in India's heartland has alienated them and pushed them closer to the left-wing guerrillas. They, one the other hand, are adept at exploiting this by presenting themselves, unlike the Indian state, as protectors of indigenous traditions.

I sought to uncover details of this overlooked aspect of the conflict in my work. Getting primary material from the ground was not easy and I spent around 15 days in very hostile terrain here. I remember how I, along with my local contact, crossed a major river on boat and then drove on a motorbike through dirt track in thick forests to try and meet the guerrillas. It didn't work out in the end despite initial overtures but I did meet some Maoists who had surrendered at a local police station to get details of their linguistic work.

Often, I found myself in very depressing and forsaken towns. At night, in my dingy and crummy hotel rooms, I would question myself what I was doing. But the pursuit of new information kept me going. I felt vindicated when I managed to lay my hands on textbooks as well as medical and botanical manuals produced by the education and literary wing of the

Maoists. That was the first time anybody from the media managed to bring them to the fore to show the guerrillas had indeed worked better than state to protect indigenous knowledge and traditions.

This is an issue I am very passionate about and it is one of my niche expertise domains. I would advise young professionals to try and identify their niche domains as early as possible in their career and develop deeper knowledge in them along the way. This is something that requires commitment as well as patience because it may not yield short-term benefits but sets you apart in the crowd in the long run.

Editor's Note: Debarshi's penchant and flair for in-depth, human interest stories can be easily glimpsed even from his newspaper pieces. As India correspondent for The Straits Times, he recently wrote a piece on the Myanmar refugees in India's Mizoram. Here is an extract from the piece which gives one a strong sense of his writing style.

"Mr Lalzachhuana cleans his solar panel lovingly, using a damp cloth to wipe the dust off its surface. It is a luxury for his displaced family who are now forced to live in a ramshackle blue tarpaulin shelter at a refugee camp in Zokhawthar, an Indian town in Mizoram and on the border with Myanmar. The panel powers a light bulb and allows them to charge their mobile phones. But this small mercy nearly cost Mr Lalzachhuana, who goes by one name, his life. When the 63-year-old went back to his house in New Haimual in Chin state to retrieve the panel on Jan 29 – the day he and his family hurriedly crossed over into India fearing a clash between the Myanmar army and opposing groups – he walked straight into a skirmish. He hid in a culvert, clinging on to his panel and praying for his dear life, as bullets whizzed past above him. 'I told myself I was going to die because of the panel,' said Mr Lalzachhuana. 'I really regretted going back.' Still fearful of further clashes, he is in no hurry to return. 'If God permits, I hope we can go back next year but right now it (my home) feels quite far,' he said, gesturing to a hill in the backdrop in Myanmar. His house, he added, is just beyond it. Two small rectangular patches of red chillies lay drying near his tent – part of the meagre possessions

the family brought with them in this indefinite period of exile. A year on since the coup, the humanitarian crisis in Myanmar still remains on the boil, with people like Mr Lalzachhuana and his family spilling over into Mizoram from time to time in search of refuge. Around 5,000 arrived in this eastern Indian state in the last week of January, taking up the number of displaced Myanmar nationals in Mizoram to more than 20,000. It helps that the 404 km Indo-Myanmar border in Mizoram is porous, with the two countries separated just by the meandering Tiau river at Zokhawthar that locals walk across in dry months."

Following a stint as Senior Policy Advisor on political, media and cultural affairs with the New Zealand High Commission in New Delhi from March 2014 to May 2018, you went back to journalism and are now working as India Correspondent for The Straits Times. In this role, you offer readers glimpses of the country and its people. Looking at human interest stories in particular, can you, citing examples, give us an idea of how you chase them and the curiosity and drive often needed to bring them to life?

Editor's Note: For the Covid 19 pandemic in India, for instance, Debarshi has penned heartwrenching pieces focusing on people – families allowed to bury the dead in backyards amidst overwhelmed crematoriums; kindness of strangers in the face of horrors;journalists paying a price for their coverage; and the plight of the so-called pandemic 'tiger widows'.

"The job of the newspaper is to comfort the afflicted and afflict the comfortable" – this is what was drilled into us while studying at journalism school. And this is something that still serves as a lodestar for me nearly two decades into my career. I always try to report on the impact people have to bear in their daily lives from wider events. These seemingly complex macro phenomena, such as inflation or unemployment, become more accessible when journalists are able to humanise them – that is find people who encapsulate the wider trend we seek to report on. It makes the subject more accessible and relatable to readers, I feel.

For instance, the negative economic fallout of the pandemic and jobless migrants are subjects we have been writing about constantly. However, I took that a step further in my story through the pandemic's tiger widows. It came about because I had read about returning out-of-work migrants, those who had returned to the Sundarbans and were being killed by tigers after being forced to venture deeper into the jungles. I had reported on tiger widows in the past and reactivated my network to try and trace families of recent migrant workers who had been killed by tigers. It took several calls and patience to find such families. Doing so over the phone is not always easy as one has to chase people (who evidently have far more important things to do than help demanding journalists!). But I also needed to find case studies before travelling to ensure the long trip was not futile.

Finding the right families is just one challenge though. To get these widows who have been through a lot and narrated their ordeal multiple times over to many government officials as well as journalists – that is another battle. Often you find them not willing to speak, which is a natural fallout from the lack of support from state and other agencies. "How will I benefit by narrating my sorrow to you? I don't want to waste my time." That is something I often have to hear while reporting in the field. I tell them that I am here to do my job, which is to report about their plight and tell others about it. That many have benefited from generous readers who sent in money to support individuals after reading about them in my report has been really uplifting. It motivates me to keep writing about the marginalised. One such reader sent in money for the four widows mentioned in my story. I hope it has changed their opinion about journalism and its impact.

Next let's go back a little to get an idea how all this – your affair with the business of communication – started. You went to The Scindia School, an Indian boarding school for boys, and then studied journalism, political science and economics at the Delhi College of Arts and Commerce. Can you give us a sense of your upbringing in terms of how the environment and the people around you shaped your development? In particular, please share

how traits valued in your career – eg drive, stamina, sense of wonder, affinity for the marginalized etc – were either encouraged or potentially undermined knowingly or unknowingly, and how you have, in a way, emerged somewhat unscathed?

I was born into and grew up in a household that respected literature and the art of writing. As a child, my parents and my grandmother (my father's mother who lived with us) introduced me to the magical world of Bengali and English children's literature. My grandmother had a particular formative influence on me because she taught me how to read and write in Bengali (a language I did not learn at school because I lived in Assam, where Assamese, along with Hindi and English, was taught to children at most schools). Besides listening to her read me the classics, I would read out Bengali language texts, including newspapers, at a later stage to her. This sealed my lifelong-affair with the written word as well as love for learning languages.

Even the otherwise ramshackle school that I first went to, one run by a dedicated Anglo-Indian couple, primed books. I still cherish a Brer Rabbit storybook (one which I still have) that I received as a prize after coming first in class. It was with this literary background that I went into one of India's finest schools, which further sharpened my interest in reading and writing. My teachers at Scindia School encouraged me to get into debates, plays, elocution and writing, all of which I took part in with delight. My principal Mr Dar deserves to be recognised. He encouraged us to read beyond what we were expected to study for our classwork. It was he who pushed and inspired me to read novels, edit the school's fortnightly, pursue photography and participate in theatre. He was also the one who sent me on an exchange to a German school. Indeed, he did all that and so much more to lay the foundation for the person I am today.

Another person who shaped my early career is Srinjoy Chowdhury who in the early 2000s was heading the features section of The Statesman newspaper in Delhi. That was where I interned while studying journalism at college. He spotted the talent I had for reporting and writing and encouraged me to work on longer stories that often formed the cover for the newspaper's weekend supplement. I remember certain photographers were not happy that I took pictures for my stories (using the SLR camera my parents bought me while at school) but Srinjoy did not ask me to back down. That initial push and support early in my journalism career proved incredibly valuable and inspiring.

I also grew up in tea estates, which are home to many workers from communities that are known as "tea tribes". They are descendants of indigenous tribal communities who were brought into Assam from other parts of the country in the 19th century. Some of these workers were and still are employed as domestic helpers in the manager's bungalow. I came to see them as friends, not as "servants" or "labourers" (as they were referred to by some). I spent time playing with them just as I would with other friends, even talking to them in their indigenous creole. My parents also taught me to respect them. This early egalitarian exposure ensured I grew up to rebel against class divides and to have a strong sense of affinity for the marginalised. I suppose these would be seen as inherent attributes for a good journalist.

Finally, Debarshi, much has been said about India and its cities. For instance, to quote author Mark Twain, "India is the One land that all men desire to see, and having seen once, by even a glimpse, would not give that glimpse for all the shows of all the rest of the globe combined." As for the country's capital, poet Mirza Asadullah Khan Ghalib famously noted, "One day I asked my soul: what is Delhi? She replied: The world is the body and Delhi is its soul." As someone who has grown up in India and now covers it with its warts and all, how would you, at the expense of over simplification, describe it – and distinguish the complex cities within it – to young people who are curious but know little about it?

I don't want to oversimplify because if I do so, I would be dishonest to myself and disrespectful to my country's incredible diversity. I often tell foreigners it is best to think of India as an entity similar to the European Union with the states here – each with its own kind of politics, culture and language – resembling the diverse countries that comprise the EU. That's the kind of wide-angle view one has to adopt when looking at India from outside. Just as there is no Indian cuisine (there are many kinds of Indian cuisines), the adjective "Indian" hides more than it reveals. For instance, Bollywood is often rendered as being synonymous with the Indian cinema industry. The term just refers to the Hindi film industry based in Mumbai and there are many other film industries that are based in different parts of the country, each with its own glorious traditions and millions of fans.

It is worth remembering this inherent diversity when one starts to read and learn more about India. Don't get daunted by this thought; think of it in terms of how much more there is to explore than what meets the eye and enjoy India! Certainly, there is a pan-Indian identity that has been emerging in the last two decades or so. These are individuals (at the risk of oversimplifying!) who will enjoy a Hollywood or Bollywood film as much as they will a film produced in their mother tongue or in a language that they now access because of subtitles on Amazon Prime Video or Netflix. This identity has come about because of economic liberalisation and migration within the country, the growth of mass media and popular culture as well as growing marriages outside the barriers of caste, religion and communities, among other phenomena. But such a community still remains mostly limited to India's big cities, with the vast majority still practising traditions unique to their community.

Delhi and the wider national capital territory, which I have called home since 2007, is home to many such "pan-Indian" families. It is a city whose population has grown manifold in the last 10 years with growing migration, thanks to migrants such as me. This is the same in the case of other cities, including Mumbai, Bengaluru and Hyderabad. This is what I like about the capital city – it is a cultural melting pot that represents the diversity of India. The country currently faces many challenges, including a rising and worrying trend of Hindu majoritarianism, economic slowdown and geopolitical threat that comes from its two adversarial neighbours (China and Pakistan). Despite these limiting factors, the country, with its lucrative base of hundreds of millions of middle class families and its combination of hard and soft power, is destined to play an increasingly important global role.

AFFINITY FOR THE MARGINALISED

"I also grew up in tea estates, which are home to many workers from communities that are known as 'tea tribes'. They are descendants of indigenous tribal communities who were brought into Assam from other parts of the country in the 19th century. Some of these workers were and still are employed as domestic helpers in the manager's bungalow. I came to see them as friends, not as 'servants' or 'labourers' (as they were referred to by some). I spent time playing with them just as I would with other friends, even talking to them in their indigenous creole. My parents also taught me to respect them. This early egalitarian exposure ensured I grew up to rebel against class divides and to have a strong sense of affinity for the marginalised. I suppose these would be seen as inherent attributes for a good journalist."

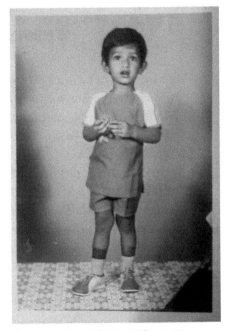

Picture courtesy of Debarshi Dasgupta

—Debarshi Dasgupta

STIRRING VOCABULARY

"As a teenager in rural 1970s Ireland, I found books unsettling. From Ernest Hemingway's Fiesta *to Laurie Lee's* As I Walked Out One Midsummer's Morning, *books suggested that 'life' lay elsewhere. The puzzling 'how' of travel came from Woody Guthrie's* Bound For Glory. *On his hitchhiking, train-hopping, Model-A Ford-riding adventures through Depression America, Guthrie survived by being a sign-writer, sailor and fruit-picker. And a musician and writer. His songs ranged from ballads to anthems, agit-prop, love lays and lullabies.* Bound for Glory *was written in a rich, demotic, playful and stirring vocabulary, as if James Joyce and John Steinbeck had collaborated with Kerouac on* On The Road. *Apparently an ability to turn one's hand to any job and strum a few chords on the guitar was the key to eating and moving, and to romance and romances. And to writing, as well. Within a month of reading* Bound for Glory, *at 17, I was away with a guitar, a sleeping bag and a notebook."*

JASPER WINN ON *BOUND FOR GLORY* BY WOODY GUTHRIE

Source: The Guardian

BORDER CITIES

Picture courtesy of Maria Siow

"Some of the more intriguing places to me are usually the border cities that China shares with countries that it has a common border with. Dongxing in Guangxi province, which borders Vietnam, is intriguing and feels very Southeast Asian to me. Apart from Chinese, signs are also written in Vietnamese and Southeast Asian products can easily be purchased here. Or Suifenhe in Heilongjiang province, which shares a common border with Russia, where you can easily buy Russian dolls, breads and vodka. Signs too are also written partly in Russian. Or Hunchun in Jilin province, which is the place to go to for a taste of both Russian and North Korean cultures/ influences. During my time in China, I have covered all regions, provinces and municipalities and all major cities. So in the more recent years, I've found myself making my way to some of the smaller cities that many may not have heard of."

—Maria Siow

CHAPTER 4

Diverse Experiences

Maria Siow
TV Correspondent/East Asia Specialist

Pictures courtesy of Maria Siow

Maria, since starting out as a journalist with The Straits Times in 1992, you have moved far and wide, joining other media outlets like Television Corporation, Channel News Asia, China's CGTV and South China Morning Post. Significantly, there were regional postings in cities like Hong Kong and Beijing. In between, you also took time off from the media scene, with a stint with Red Cross in Beijing as well as further studies in Washington and Seoul. **Broadly, what has kept you churning, so to speak, when professionals of your generation, more or less, had the option of staying put and still be well or even better rewarded, often based merely on seniority or what I will call "institutional heft"?**

Frankly, I haven't given much thought to this question but I would say the tendency to keep churning, as you put it, is due to my insatiable sense of curiosity about the world. More specifically, I am drawn to developments in East Asia. All along, the interest has been both professional and personal. I guess this is in part why the learning has been sustainable and enjoyable. For instance, I always find myself reading intensely about the region even when it is not related to work. In fact, it is a form of leisure – like bedtime reading. For example, in pursuing my interest in the Korean Peninsula, I don't just read about its general history and contemporary developments. I find myself highly interested in countless aspects such as Korean cinema and Korean literature as well. I also go into more obscure areas like the history of Korean jurisprudence and how Confucianism has evolved in the country since the start of the Chosun Dynasty in 1392.

Another reason I have been moving is I am driven mainly by the acquisition of knowledge and diverse experiences. This means more to me than acquiring what you call "institutional heft". For professionals of my generation, staying put in one place can mean the perks of seniority, which often come with monetary rewards. In life, there are trade-offs. For me, the gains that come from moving around more than compensate for whatever I might lose in doing so.

When I started my first job upon graduation, I thought The Straits Times would be my employer for life. If you had told me then that I would have gone on to such diverse places and experiences, I wouldn't have believed you. Looking back, my career trajectory has been totally unexpected. Yet one of the things that I can say with absolute certainty is I did what I really wanted to do. I followed my heart at every stage and gained a tremendous amount of satisfaction in the process. I don't think there was ever a dull moment.

Next, let's get some glimpses of your growing up years – as a child, in primary/ secondary schools and junior college (JC) as well as in university. If someone were to revisit your past, would he or she be surprised by the eventual arc of your career? Or would it be deemed expected, given your history? I refer not only to the field you have ventured into – communications broadly – but also your personal temperament (eg appetite for change and diversity).

These are interesting questions for me. I would imagine that anyone who knew me in my teens would probably write me off as a semi-failure. Sure, I attended a relatively good school (CHIJ) all the way but I was mediocre in primary school and horrendous in secondary school. This was partly because of the family problems I had during my teenage years. I skipped classes, played truant, hardly studied and was mostly distracted. I am glad I grew up in those less high-tech days when teenage mischief wasn't so easily tracked.

My O-level results were so lacking in promise that I did not qualify for a junior college or most of the courses in the polytechnics. In the end, the only option left for me was to enter one of the pre-university centers where I had to spend three years to prepare for the GCE "A" levels. It was demoralizing as the proportion of students who made it to universities from such centers was depressingly low then. I remember being unhappy during most of those three years.

But looking back, it probably wasn't such a bad thing. Being at the bottom has an uncanny way of putting things in perspective. For example, because of this formative setback, I have never allowed subsequent accolades and achievements to get too much into my head. The experience has sort of kept me rooted.

What also made a difference at the pre-university center I attended was a Chinese teacher Madam Tan Choo Siang who saw the sparkle in me that I never knew was there. She noticed my flair for both Chinese and English and encouraged me to keep writing. One of the things she said which left an indelible mark on me was "不要浪费你的才华" (which means "do not waste your talent"). I shared with her about my desire to be a correspondent in the future and she actually believed I could achieve my dream one day. And she was right. Without her belief in me, I don't think I would have walked the path I have taken.

Having lived in different cities, what – at a personal level – would be some of your strongest impressions of them generally?

That's really hard to say. A lot had to do with the stage of my life and frame of mind when I was living in those cities. Take Hong Kong, for example, where I lived for a year in 1998. I was much younger over two decades ago and game for new adventures. So everything then about the Special Administrative Region was interesting, refreshing and exciting. But when I returned to the former British colony in 2020, much of the initial allure and excitement had dissipated. It was replaced by the widened horizons gained from the many years I spent in Beijing, where domestic and international issues are viewed through much wider perspectives. Seen through the lenses of 2020, HK issues appeared parochial to me. Its importance within mainland China – which has become progressively stronger, wealthier and more influential – somewhat appeared less significant.

OK, let's take a look at your career, starting with how you started with journalism in The Straits Times. Was being a journalist a natural progression since you studied Philosophy and Political Science at the National University of Singapore? What other options were at play before you decided on ST?

Actually I am not sure the subjects one studies matter that much. For me, what made a difference were: One, I had wanted to be a journalist since I was very young – after I finished my O levels. Two, I had some freelancing jobs related to journalism during my pre-university days, thanks to the late

Mr Ee Boon Lee, who was the former editor of NTUC News and Petir. He was an excellent mentor who opened doors for me even when I was just a student. The freelance work I did for him whetted my appetite and further sealed my interest in being a journalist.

So when I eventually entered university, it probably came as no surprise that I was involved in The Ridge, the campus newspaper, as well as a whole host of campus publications such as Le Message and Demos – publications of the Political Association and the Democratic Socialist Club, respectively. In my final year, there was little doubt that I wanted to be a full-fledged journalist. I did not even think about other options.

I wanted to work in The Straits Times. So Singapore Press Holdings was the only place that I sent an application to. Prior to my final examinations in NUS, I went for an interview with ST where I came face to face with veterans Patrick Daniel and the late Felix Soh. Felix asked me which desk I wanted to work for. "Either the newsdesk or the political desk," I said without hesitation. I was offered a job soon after. Felix told me that he was happy with my answer. He said: "Way too many new graduates want to write for Life to cover the arts, to do travel writing and so on...Come on, we have to cover the news. News is the bread and butter of ST."

Your stint at ST was relatively brief – about two years. Yet you have described this period as "a steep learning curve." How so and why?

Upon arriving in ST, I was put on the political desk which came as a surprise to me. Most rookies then were placed on the news desk or crime desk. The political desk, as I knew it, was usually reserved for senior and more experienced journalists. I soon realized that I was put on the desk due to my good command of the Chinese language. You see, I started work in May 1992. The year before, if you recall, PAP lost four constituencies to the opposition. The loss was blamed on PAP "losing touch with the Chinese ground and the HDB heartland". Issues like not having enough places to burn joss papers during the Seventh Month cropped up. They reportedly turned the Chinese ground "against the PAP". There was the sense that ST was too much of an "anglophile". It was also getting too elitist. Some pointed to the coverage of stories such as country club disputes as a sign that the paper was losing touch with ordinary residents living in the heartlands.

In those years, few ST journalists were good in Chinese, and those who were either covered culture or entertainment. So the political desk started to take in bilingual rookies, which was how I ended up there. Sure enough, it was a steep learning curve for a young graduate. Suddenly I had to understand issues quickly and learn how to ask politicians, trade unionists, clan association elders and community leaders questions while grappling with the complexities of prevailing issues. I also had to get over my initial apprehension about approaching people to ask for quotes. I had to learn how to listen to what people had to say in order to ask good follow-up questions. I had my fair share of blunders. One was so classic that I am sure former colleagues will still remember it today.

You then moved to Television Corporation of Singapore where you were first senior broadcast journalist (May 1994 to December 1997) and then Hong Kong correspondent (January 1998 to February 1999). Can you share about your transition from print to TV and radio? Also, how about the move from covering Singapore to covering Hong Kong? What were some challenges and what kind of mindset proved helpful?

Editor's Note: As senior broadcast journalist, Maria covered for television national and community issues, parliamentary sittings, select committee hearings, speeches by top politicians and local politics. She covered the 1997 General Election and was on major overseas trips involving leaders like Prime Minister Goh Chok Tong and Senior Minister Lee Kuan Yew. As Hong Kong correspondent, she reported on social, economic, political and business news in the Special Administrative Region. Notable events included the financial crisis and economic downturn affecting life in the SAR and the unprecedented intervention in the stock market by the SAR government.

I left ST for a range of reasons related to youthful angst, unhappiness with the way I was managed and the perception I had then of having a difficult boss. Today, after close to three decades of working, I am almost angst-free when it comes to work. So I invariably look back at my younger self with a large dose of amusement and a not insignificant measure of loathing. Looking back, I was too young to see things from a manager's perspective. Now, having managed younger colleagues in the course of my career, I can understand better the challenges and difficulties of leading people.

After I left ST, I had the chance to join Petroleum Argus as a journalist covering the oil and petroleum sector. It was offering me significantly more than what I was getting at ST. But TCS was also hiring and I found myself being offered the post of current affairs producer, which paid me less. I chose the latter as I thought it would be more interesting. I guess I was proven right. I spent eight months in Talking Point learning about television production. I produced current affairs segments for the show and learnt the difference between writing for print and television. I was lucky to get to attend single-camera courses and even a course on studio basics where I learnt how to be a studio director. Once I even doubled up as the studio director for an episode. I felt sweat sticking to my shirt. My hair was dripping wet after the session was over, even though the air conditioner was on full blast. Being in the studio director's seat was that intense.

I left the current affairs team to join the first TCS political desk. The desk had Yeo Hock Lin (the political editor), Lee Foong Ming, Wong Shuk Min, Debra Soon, Jane Lau and myself. Among us, we covered the major political news in Singapore, went on ministerial walkabouts, reported on national day speeches and rallies, and even covered many overseas trips involving then Prime Minister Goh Chok Tong, Senior Minister Lee Kuan Yew and other ministers. Along the way, my voice was cleared for voicing and I appeared on television doing standups. I think I was really stiff and uncomfortable in my early standups!

After about five years of covering the political beat, I was given the opportunity to head to Hong Kong. At that time, TCS only had two regional bureaus – Hong Kong and Bangkok – and my predecessor Angela Ee was calling it quits shortly after the Hong Kong handover. I jumped at the opportunity as it meant new challenges.

What kind of mindset saw me through those transitions? I guess the biggest would be versatility. I have never wanted to become a TV journalist appearing upfront. In the old days of local TV, this would not have been possible anyway. But there was greater media liberalization. There was also a new CEO brought in from outside. He believed in seeing more faces on air, especially those of journalists who were out there getting the news and writing their own stories and PTC (piece to camera) lines. In the past, those in front of the cameras were news readers whose job was to read the news or appear on location looking picture-perfect and reading perfectly-delivered lines pre-written by someone else.

Another important mindset is the constant quest for new challenges. If I hadn't taken up the HK posting, I am not sure how long I could have continued covering political news for TV before I got tired of it or felt that I was not learning new things. The HK posting opened up a much broader and wider canvas for me, not just in journalism but also in knowledge acquisition. By then, I had come to sense that Singapore news and issues, while important on the island, must go with other weighty and substantive issues out there which had a bearing on us, given our interconnected world.

Then came the period TV viewers interested in current affairs will associate you with most – the time when you were China correspondent and then China bureau chief with Channel News Asia, from February 1999 to January 2005. This was an intense period, with many highlights. Looking back, how would you describe your experience as China correspondent and bureau chief? Was it hard having to cover in both English and Chinese? How about having to cater to both news bulletins and current affairs programs, including documentaries – given how the treatment for them is very different? What kind of adjustments were needed to do a good job?

Editor's Note: *Among notable events Maria covered were Premier Zhu Rongji's visit to the United States in 1999, China's reaction to NATO's bombing of the Chinese embassy in Belgrade and China's 50th National Day celebrations. Also covered were China's successful bid of the 2008 Olympic Games, its debut in the 2002 World Cup and North Korean refugees seeking asylum in its diplomatic compounds.*

I think what stood out initially for me were the difficulties and challenges – administratively, technically etc – of setting up the Channel News Asia Beijing bureau from scratch. When I first arrived in Beijing in 1999, I faced the immediate constraints of not having an office space and basic things such as furniture, telephone lines and equipment. So everything had to begin from scratch, including registering with the Chinese ministry overseeing any foreign bureau's presence in China – in this case, the Ministry of Foreign Affairs. I had to surmount all kinds of initial problems. For instance, I had to find out where and how much it would cost to rent camera equipment, and familiarize myself with the technical process of sending and editing visuals/stories back to Singapore via satellite transmission.

When things were a little more settled, I had to facilitate the bureaucracy and tackle other tasks – hire a camera crew, an office assistant and a driver; purchase the bureau vehicle; renovate the bureau to make sure that it had a suitable backdrop/studio and setup for live transmissions. The work was new and endless. And all this was carried out against the backdrop of operating in a foreign environment where efficiency and ways to get things done were very different from what I was accustomed to in Singapore. Apart from this being yet another steep learning curve, it was a quick way in learning how to operate in China – with different approaches and communication methods needed in different settings when relating to different people. Even so, my expectations had to be moderated. I also needed to have a massive amount of patience.

Editorially, I had to quickly familiarise myself with issues in a rapidly evolving China – a process which took many years (and is still a work in progress). This was daunting given how diverse China is and how complex its issues are. I had to get to know people fast and put myself on email lists of events and press conferences. At times I even had to explain to newsmakers what CNA was. It was then a new regional outfit and totally unheard of.

I also had to grapple with a bureaucracy that could hardly be described as cooperative when it came to facilitating the work of foreign journalists. Indeed, many officials saw the foreign media as adversaries. They had little idea what foreign journalists wanted or were interested in. Another problem with the bureaucracy was that it tended to view CNA as a national broadcaster of Singapore and hence it must toe the Chinese line, as "China has good relations with Singapore". So any efforts in pursuing stories contrary to this line of thinking will invite questions. Once my cameraman and I were detained by security forces for trying to film the exterior of China's anti-corruption bureau "without permission" for a story on anti-corruption.

Even some ordinary people appear to be suspicious of the foreign media. Once I wanted to interview a household on ways the residents had undertaken to conserve water, such as saving water by reusing water used for washing their food/rice/vegetables to flush their toilets, for a story on how different societies were coping with water shortages – a global issue and challenge. But one of the first things the matriarch of the household asked me was: "Why are you doing this story? Are you trying to portray China as a county where we don't have enough water and its people are poor? Are you out to make China look bad?"

Looking back, I think I spent virtually all my waking hours on work – preparing, reading, overcoming the various administrative and logistical challenges in order to get my job done. But it was an exhilarating experience for me, being able to finally get a seat where I could view up close China's phenomenal changes and rapid developments. There was never a dull moment being in a country as vast and complex as China, especially since I also had the chance to travel widely throughout the country. By the end of my second stint in China, I had visited all 31 Chinese provinces, municipalities and autonomous regions.

Covering in both languages was not difficult as I am comfortable writing in English and Chinese. But doing standups in Chinese took some getting used to. Doing standups on the streets of Beijing invariably invited onlookers, the majority of whom would not understand what I said in English. But when I spoke in Chinese, people understood. Apart from making sure that my choice of words was measured and accurate, I made it a point not to take up too much time. I didn't want to invite excessive attention or scrutiny, especially from old ladies wearing red armbands who had the authority to force you to leave, even if you were in a public area.

I think one of the most important mindsets to have is to never think that one knows it all. In fact, the longer I stay in China and outside of Singapore generally, the more I have learnt that there are still so many gaps in knowledge. I guess it helps to always be modest, curious and insatiable. Keep on asking "why" instead of expounding on what one knows. I always tell people that the more time I spend in China, the less certain I am of anything I know due to the country's fast changing nature. Again, this sort of keeps one rooted.

Between 2005 and 2007, you took time off from the media scene to pursue Korean Studies at Yonsei University and then a Masters in International Public Policy and Practice at George Washington University's Elliott School of International Affairs. What led you to postgraduate studies in South Korea and USA? Looking back, how has this foray into the academic realm made a difference subsequently in terms of your career and your development as a journalist?

In Korea, I pursued Korean Studies and International Affairs. My interest in acquiring more knowledge about the Korean Peninsula was triggered by two chief developments. The first was my one-week assignment to the Hermit Kingdom in 2002 which was a fascinating peek into the secretive nation. The second was the slew of North Korean-related stories that I had to cover in the course of my work, especially the increase in the number of North Koreans seeking asylum in foreign – mainly South Korean and

Japanese – embassies in Beijing. In those years, many of these refugees made their way across the North Korean border to China in a bid to escape hunger, persecution or both. Or they wanted to rejoin their relatives who had escaped North Korea. I was deeply curious about the context and history that had compelled them to make the dangerous and arduous trip to what would be a highly uncertain future.

I think that was the period before the Korean wave hit Singapore and other parts of Asia. Though I had watched some Korean drama series, my interest in the Korean Peninsula was chiefly in its contemporary developments and its history dating back to the start of the Chosun Dynasty. After six years as China correspondent and bureau chief for CNA, I thought it was time to take a break to recharge my batteries.

I first went to Yonsei but later put in an application to the Elliott School in GWU. I chose Elliot not just because it is one of the best schools in the world to study international relations. It also has an excellent course and faculty when it comes to East Asia. But since I had to wait to see if my application was successful, I stayed on in Yonsei for another semester. That was when I really enjoyed my classes, especially those on Korean Law & Politics and Korean Confucianism – both of which were taught by the erudite, brilliant and scholarly Professor Chaihark Hahm.

In both Yonsei and GWU, I acquired deeper knowledge and understanding about East Asian issues and developments. In GWU, I also had the chance to attend many of the talks, seminars and discussions in Washington DC and listen to the countless academics, analysts, advocates and activists share their knowledge and expertise on a wide range of global issues and challenges. It was an unbelievably eye opening and intellectual stimulating experience, to say the least. Both places have added depth and given me greater skills to carry on my job as a journalist. Without the extra effort to acquire in-depth knowledge, it is sometimes hard to understand beyond the headlines and developments to answer the bigger questions related to the "whys" and "hows".

Following that "academic detour", you came back to journalism and was East Asia Bureau Chief at Channel NewsAsia from February 2008 to November 2012. **What was the challenge in broadening your scope to cover not only China (already vast) but also East Asia in general? Also was there a shift in the way you did your job after the strengthening of your academic grounding, given your stints in Seoul and Washington?**

Editor's Note: Working in English and Chinese, Maria covered political, economic and social developments in China – focusing on not only news but also current affairs. She travelled extensively within China and visited Mongolia and North Korea on reporting assignments.

Coming back to the CNA bureau in Beijing again with a broader mandate, so to speak, was an exhilarating experience. I went to North Korea again on assignments and travelled to Mongolia too to cover stories. I think the second stint meant that I was able to find more of the jig-saw puzzle pieces which I found missing during my first stint due to my gaps of knowledge in understanding China.

The ability to pull in the different strands of knowledge to understand the broader picture really helped in the second stint. For example, the key to understanding China's environmental problems lies not just in understanding the environmental dimensions, even though these are certainly important. It also lies in understanding the politics of it all, especially at the provincial and county levels. There local bureaucrats are assessed based on how much they have contributed to the area's economy in terms of output, GNP and investments – not on how well they have maintained the rivers and kept them free of pollutants.

During this period, you had a chance to serve as Visiting Fellow at East-West Center in Washington, from August 2010 to December 2010. You did research into the debates on China's soft power among Chinese analysts, academics and commentators, giving an update on the progress and development of Confucius Institutes worldwide, including their hits and misses. **How useful**

was a stint in a global think tank – with its opportunity for reflection and intellectual engagement – for your professional development?

It was certainly very useful in giving me access to certain talks and discussions that may not be open to the public, such as those at Rand and the Center for Strategic and International Studies. Again, the intellectual stimulation was unbeatable and bridged the gap between what some say is the superficiality of the media and the depth and rigours of academia and think tanks. I don't buy this simplistic distinction for I think good journalism can have depth too. So it is all the more important that I have some exposure to the academic circle to lend credibility to my stance.

Then came what I would consider an interesting shift – your stint with the International Committee of the Red Cross as East Asia Regional Analyst based in Beijing between December 2012 and January 2015. How did the opportunity at Red Cross come about and did this job represent a new form of learning for you since you took it up "in search of varied professional experience"?

Editor's Note: At the ICRC, Maria prepared country reports and analytical updates on potential situations of conflict in mainly China and North Korea as well as developments in South Korea and Mongolia. In her role as regional analyst, she also examined China's foreign policy and global influence in countries such as Afghanistan, North Korea and South Sudan.

It (the chance to work for Red Cross) was rather unexpected actually. I met the ICRC head of East Asia delegation at an official engagement in Beijing. He was interested in my background and asked if I was keen to work as an East Asia researcher/analyst for them. Since this was the first and only non-media related job I had taken up, it was extremely eye-opening to get a glimpse into how an international NGO operates, its constraints, and even quirks and eccentricities. As an organisation that seeks to, among other things, resolve international armed conflicts and promote international humanitarian laws around the world, it – similar to diplomacy perhaps – does its work in a way that is away from the public eye and largely beyond the media glare.

I experienced first hand the contrast from the media. For example, some of my most thoughtful papers and essays written in ICRC were read only by a small group of colleagues internally. In contrast, some of the media pieces which I wrote which I wouldn't care to read again were widely read, shared and even critiqued and torn apart for nuances which may or may not have been intended. The two-week training that I received in Geneva was also invaluable. I gained a lot of knowledge regarding the Red Cross and Red Crescent movements, ways to operate and even stay alive in a hostile/hostage environment, human rights, humanitarian laws, negotiation and diplomacy skills.

After the Red Cross stint, you went back very briefly to CNA as East Asia Senior Correspondent before becoming International (Asia) Planning Editor (from November 2016 to April 2020) at CGTN in Beijing. This "big picture" role involved programme planning as well as planning for special events and projects. It also included management of staff and work flow as well as editorial, production and technical issues. In addition, you conducted writing workshops for writers and producers and reviewed the standards of the English translations of Chinese films, documentaries and dramas. How will you place your role at CGTN in Beijing – which was varied and involved more people management compared to your earlier professional roles – in your overall learning space?

In CGTN, I was officially a planner for Asian news. This meant I helped to decide on the stories that went into the daily Asian bulletin. I was also involved in mid-term and long-term plans regarding stories and angles we should go for. In addition, I commissioned stories and series ahead of major news events such as those related to APEC and BRICS. But what I hadn't expected about the role was that it also allowed me to interact with the large numbers of aspiring, smart and motivated young Chinese in the newsroom. I found myself invariably being a mentor to some of these writers, video editors, line producers and reporters. Prior to this job, I had never thought of myself much as a mentor. But this job allowed me not only to discover but also to enjoy this new role. It gave me immense satisfaction to watch some of these young people grow professionally and gain more confidence.

Unlike my time as a correspondent, this was also the first time that I was mainly desk-bound in my job. This allowed me to finally see and further appreciate the role of the output/production team back at base, something which I had probably taken for granted when I was a correspondent. I began to appreciate certain challenges more deeply – eg how to fill up airtime with interesting stories and information in a multimedia format. I also came to understand all the fastidiousness about keeping to strict timings and durations in a live-cross (so that you don't over run and "ruin" the rest of the line-up in the nicely-put-together bulletin).

You have joined South China Morning Post as Senior Asia Correspondent since June 2020. In this role, you write news articles, updates, features, analysis and opinion pieces on "China's diplomacy, footprints and interactions in the region, especially Southeast Asia and East Asia, and the evolving strategic, security and geopolitical landscape in the Asia-Pacific region." After so many years, how do you keep yourself motivated and refreshed as "media specialist, China specialist, East Asia specialist, East Asia regional analyst, journalist, correspondent, researcher, writer, columnist, communicator"?

I think there is a part of me that is never truly satisfied with the current state of affairs. I want to keep on moving and trying out new things. For the longest time, CNA enabled me to do that as I started as a young journalist there. So moving up the ranks or around the organisation was not hard. But as one moves further up the professional ladder at least in terms of years of experience, the ability to move to newer challenges within the same organization becomes increasingly harder. Perhaps that is why the search for varied experiences often has to come in the form of different and multiple jobs and organizations. I hope and am convinced that I will never reach the stage where I feel I've known "enough". I don't want to stop learning new things. I don't want to cease being curious. I hope this insatiable thirst for knowledge and curiosity in me will never die out. Otherwise it is time to ship out.

Editor's Note: *Maria's passion for her job remains strong in part because it gives her a platform to ask probing questions. Take, for instance, a piece she wrote for The South China Morning Post in December 2021 questioning the silence of the US on Myanmar's Rohingya – more so as it cries "genocide" at China for Xinjiang. She writes pointedly:"Why has the* United States *not accused* Myanmar *of committing genocide against its Rohingya Muslim minority, almost a year after saying the same of China and its Uygur Muslims in* Xinjiang? *Given that the grim details of both countries' alleged abuses against their respective minority groups emerged in 2017, the lack of censure from Washington as it drags its heels on condemning Naypyidaw is rather unfathomable. Last week, US Secretary of State Antony Blinken said during a visit to the region that Washington was looking 'actively' at whether actions taken in Myanmar might constitute genocide. I am not sure what there is to look at, much less 'actively', given that thousands of Rohingya were killed by Myanmar troops after a brutal military crackdown in August 2017. Nearly 1 million Rohingya subsequently fled Myanmar's Rakhine state to take refuge in neighbouring Bangladesh. Myanmar faces genocide charges in several international courts and a United Nations fact-finding mission even described the killings as a 'textbook example of ethnic cleansing and slow-burning genocide'. Apart from abducting and raping women and girls, the report noted that soldiers had piled bodies in at least five mass graves before burning their faces off with acid. An estimated 24,000 Rohingya have been killed, according to an Ontario International Development Agency report, with 34,000 more thrown into fires, 114,000 beaten and 18,000 women and girls raped. What more evidence does Washington want?"*

On the flip side, she has questioned the Chinese in another SCMP piece published in March 2022. Wondering if a condescending approach towards other regional countries will take China's diplomacy far, she writes: "One theme stood out for me while listening to a press conference this week by Foreign Minister Wang Yi. And that is China's apparent world view that countries in the region are not quite capable of making their own decisions and often subjected to the 'interference' of others. Replying to a question on India-China relations,

Wang said 'some forces have always sought to stoke tension between China and India'. In response to whether China and Asean countries can overcome their differences and reach a code of conduct on the South China Sea, Wang warned the regional grouping to 'firmly thwart disturbances' from countries outside the region who do not wish to see tranquillity in the disputed waters. 'Asean countries need to stay clear-eyed about this and jointly resist disturbances and sabotage attempts from outside', Wang said on the sidelines of the National People's Congress, referring to the United States and its allies. While these are fairly standard answers in Chinese foreign policy postures, I am not sure if diplomats realise such responses appear patronising, even condescending.It is as if regional countries do not know any better about making independent foreign policy choices.....Countries are naturally guided by national interests and this needs no reminders or sermonising from a country which is the most influential economic power but yet also induces the most discomfort in the region. Instead of engaging in 'condescension diplomacy', it is better for China to address Southeast Asia's discomfort with its policies, such as the use of economic tools to punish a country's foreign policy choice, or its strong-arm tactics in the South China Sea and the Mekong River."

You have spent a large part of your career in China, based in the city of Beijing in particular. This is a privilege as it has meant a ringside seat to witness the unprecedented social and economic changes sweeping through the country. In a twist to Steve Jobs' "stay hungry, stay foolish" mantra, one might imagine the need to "stay curious" in particular in your case. Looking back, what, to you, has been most intriguing about China and its cities?

This is really hard to answer as China is so vast and complex and sometimes defies categorisation. Some of the more intriguing places to me are usually the border cities that China shares with countries that it has a common border with. Dongxing in Guangxi province, which borders Vietnam, is intriguing and feels very Southeast Asian to me. Apart from Chinese, signs are also written in Vietnamese and Southeast Asian products can easily be purchased here. Or Suifenhe in Heilongjiang province, which shares a common border with Russia, where you can easily buy Russian dolls, breads and vodka. Signs too are also written partly in Russian. Or Hunchun in Jilin province, which is the place to go to for a taste of both Russian and North Korean cultures/influences. During my time in China, I have covered all regions, provinces and municipalities and all major cities. So in the more recent years, I've found myself making my way to some of the smaller cities that many may not have heard of.

When I started my first stint in China in the late 90s, I disliked travelling by train as it was slow, uncomfortable and the toilets (mostly) dirty. But in recent years, with the introduction of high-speed rail which are cleaner and more comfortable, not to mention faster, many smaller cities have become more easily accessible. Before relocating to Hong Kong in 2020 and before Covid made travelling difficult, I remember revisiting many of the places I used to visit in the past (such as Wuhan and Changchun), and checking out new but smaller cities/counties such as Lanling, Gaomi, Weifang and Linyi in Shandong province (Shandong is one of the nearest provinces to Beijing, apart from Hebei, so most destinations there can now be reached in a few hours via high-speed rail). These places all have distinct characters. For example, Gaomi was the birthplace of Mo Yan, Nobel Prize winner for Chinese Literature, while Weifang is known as the city of kites.

Finally, Maria, looking back, what would you say are some traits that might have given you an edge in the competitive market place? Your willingness to explore new opportunities? The fact that you are effectively bilingual? Your curiosity? Your temperament which has helped you deal with uncertainty and pressure? Overall, what is your advice to young professionals?

I think it is good not to expect that the next job one takes will always be grander, more "important" or better in terms of pay. For me, it is always okay and even desirable not to be bureau chief or a manager tasked to manage more people. It is okay too to take a slight pay cut. This "frees" you to concentrate on other important attributes of a job which will help you grow professionally. Yes, money and career advancement in the traditional sense are not unimportant. But looking back, they hadn't been my first considerations when I changed jobs. There were always other factors at play, including personal ones.

It is also realistic to expect that, over the years, most if not all of your bosses or managers are going to be younger than you. The other qualities you have mentioned certainly matter too. They include, for instance, the willingness to explore new opportunities and being effectively bilingual. For me, being bilingual has opened doors, especially given China's growing importance and international stature in recent years. Of course, having a temperament which has helped me in dealing with uncertainties and pressure is useful too. Indeed, being able to keep cool under duress, which is an essential quality in live television, has made a world of difference in my case.

DISTINCT CHARACTERS

Picture courtesy of Maria Siow

"When I started my first stint in China in the late 90s, I disliked travelling by train as it was slow, uncomfortable and the toilets (mostly) dirty. But in recent years, with the introduction of high-speed rail which are cleaner and more comfortable, not to mention faster, many smaller cities have become more easily accessible. Before relocating to Hong Kong in 2020 and before Covid made travelling difficult, I remember revisiting many of the places I used to visit in the past (such as Wuhan and Changchun), and checking out new but smaller cities/counties such as Lanling, Gaomi, Weifang and Linyi in Shandong province (Shandong is one of the nearest provinces to Beijing, apart from Hebei, so most destinations there can now be reached in a few hours via high-speed rail). These places all have distinct characters. For example, Gaomi was the birthplace of Mo Yan, Nobel Prize winner for Chinese Literature, while Weifang is known as the city of kites."

—Maria Siow

"IN BETWEEN" PLACES

"Pico Iyer was the writer who showed me how to take the Open Road (also the title of his sublime study of the Dalai Lama). Iyer's cultural and spiritual quest is driven by his own hybridity. Of all his books, it was The Global Soul *that felt like the blow to the head I needed in 2001, when grappling with my own cultural and spiritual alienation. It's a book that launches the 21st century, and if this sounds grand, he is grand. In* The Global Soul *he goes to 'in-between' places – airports, malls, the no-place of jet lag – and introduces the species of soul who has multiple passports, lives in several countries, and has nightmares not of the 'Where am I?' variety, but of the more neurotically advanced 'Who am I?' kind."*

KAPKA KASSABOVA ON *THE GLOBAL SOUL* BY PICO IYER

Source: The Guardian

NEW RHYTHM

Picture courtesy of Walter Sim

"The thrills really come from having a ringside seat in a dynamic society that is at odds with modernity and tradition. It is also exciting to find a new rhythm to life in an entirely different country and to practise my Japanese while making mistakes along the way. As a bonus, there is the joy of travelling and finding places off the beaten track. The way many things are done in Japan will bewilder any fresh-eyed Singaporean – and that was me at first. Indeed, the dissonance was especially great in my first few months. It is once again amplified during the Covid-19 pandemic when I have been stupefied by many things. This is Japan, the land of high tech gadgets, and yet we have practical issues like its inability to use technology for contact-tracing and its need to have vaccination records that are paper-based. Things can get puzzling, to say the least.....Not knowing anyone meant I had to actively try to make friends – which was a bit of a struggle primarily because of my personality. I tend to find socialising exhausting, though I can switch on the 'network mode' for purposes of work.....Furthermore, there was the issue of language. Business Japanese is entirely different from the conversational Japanese used in day-to-day interactions. Then there was also the issue of business etiquette like how emails are written, how name cards are exchanged (with both hands), how far to bow in greeting, how formal a greeting should be and so on. Even today, I don't think I've fully grasped all these complexities."

—Walter Sim

CHAPTER 5

Inquisitive & Versatile

Walter Sim
Japan Correspondent

Pictures courtesy of Walter Sim

Walter, your LinkedIn profile has described you as an "inquisitive, versatile and global-minded communications professional with a nose for news, an eye for detail and an interest in building relationship." This has led you to where to you are now – as Japan Correspondent for The Straits Times based in Tokyo. I assume it isn't so straight forward. Growing up, you went to traditionally good schools and did well under our system which – though excellent in standard ways – isn't (or at least wasn't) very much into the very traits that have taken you far in today's workplace. Can you give us a glimpse of your early years (in primary school, secondary school, JC), with insights into your personal growth (or lack of it)? What were some obstacles you faced in terms of the development of the "wider you", given the prevailing learning climate then, and how did you get round them (if you could)?

How I wish things were that straight-forward! In reality, they weren't which meant the process involved some fumbling and all when I was growing up. Socially, I was incredibly awkward as a child – to the point where I struggled to fit in with my peers despite attending traditionally good schools. I'm not quite sure why. Perhaps it was due to some form of personal complex. As one can imagine, the good-lookers and the class clowns would be more popular. As an only child whose parents were somewhat distant and left me to my own devices, I was quite withdrawn and this could have added to my lack of confidence. But this played a part in honing my interest in reading and, by extension, global affairs. I remember spending a lot of time reading. I could recite world capitals when I was very young and would occasionally even peruse the encyclopedia. This love for words also extended to reading The Straits Times everyday as my family had a subscription.

The geekiness somewhat gave way in my secondary school years when I felt some social pressure to fit in. I decided to join Chinese Drama as an extracurricular activity. First, it seemed fun and the people in the society were close knit. Also, I felt this would help me learn communication skills and emerge somewhat from my "shell". Another factor was that I used to struggle with Mandarin and I thought surrounding myself in a Chinese-speaking environment would benefit my linguistic skills. At that point I had no idea what I wanted to do in life. I just went along with the socially-acceptable, "smartest" route that my grades allowed me to take. Being very good at rote learning and memory work, my grades were relatively good. This led me to Triple Sciences and eventually Double Maths in junior college. Needless to say, I don't remember much of what I had studied now.

I guess JC was also another turning point when I lost interest in studying despite having picked a course that required a tremendous amount of effort and practice. I thought – very wrongly – I could coast my way to good grades like before. But the wake-up call was when I nearly flunked my first year of junior college. My grades were so borderline that I was given a choice to either repeat or be promoted on the condition that I would drop one subject. I got rid of Further Maths. But while I was struggling in other subjects, I was top in my class – and occasionally my cohort as well – in General Paper, especially in essays that dealt with broader, societal issues. That would eventually be my best subject at the 'A' levels.

Even so, after graduating from JC, I had no idea what I wanted to do and decided to leave things to fate. I applied to NUS Law, NTU Communication Studies and SMU Business. I was accepted by NTU and SMU. Ultimately I was enticed by the idea of a communication degree and the prospects of working in the media industry. Admittedly, knowing what I know now, if I could turn back time, I would have chosen to read Economics or Political Science as I believe they could have opened more doors – including those in journalism.

What about your university days? In what ways were you able to develop yourself in terms of being "inquisitive, versatile and global-minded"? What opportunities did you seize and what were the main takeaways from the various experiences?

Editor's Note: As an undergraduate at NTU, Walter participated in a six-month international student exchange programme at Jönköping University in Sweden in 2009. He also took part in a one-month Global Discovery Programme in Vietnam in 2010.

I think NTU's Wee Kim Wee School of Communication and Information, by its nature, attracts people who are generally inquisitive and aware of the world outside Singapore. For students, this means an opportunity to interact with like-minded peers across various fields who are more than willing to think outside the box. From what I can recall when I was there, the course materials dealt with international issues. Students were certainly urged to probe deeply and look at issues such as media ethics through different lenses – both through the courses we took and the many assignments we had to do.

Perhaps even more memorably, I benefited from a six-month student exchange programme at the Jonkoping University in Sweden in 2009. There were some special moments. For example, as part of a course I took, I produced a live TV segment that went on air on local television. Until then I never really did have the chance to go abroad (my parents don't really like the hassle of air travel). So the exchange experience was invaluable for me to broaden my worldview. I took the chance to explore Europe widely, learning about European history and cultures. I also made some friends along the way. Having tasted the value of an exchange, I followed up on that by looking out for overseas immersion programmes. That was how I got to do the one-month immersion programme in Vietnam in 2010.

Such opportunities obviously widened my perspectives and helped me to become more globally-minded. Such a mindset was also developed in part by the nature of my internship. At the Wee Kim Wee School, students did a six-month internship as part of coursework. I was fortunate to do mine at Reuters in 2011. Apart from spending time at its Asia HQ at Science Park, the stint included working at its Singapore bureau at Marina Bay where I had a chance to report on Singapore news for an international audience. For instance, I was involved in reporting on our 2011 General Election.

Looking back, I would say active involvement in some student activities as an undergraduate certainly helped as well in my case. For example, I took on the Chief Editor role for the GO-FAR (Going Overseas For Advanced Reporting) programme. We were supposed to visit Japan but the trip was cancelled due to some hesitation and complaints from parents since it was the year of the Great East Japan earthquake, tsunami and nuclear disaster. As a result, the trip was shifted to southern Thailand, particularly the areas devastated by the 2004 tsunami. As Chief Editor, I had to oversee the entire editorial plan and the overall design for the eventual publication.

All this meant there was a sharp learning curve and I found myself being thrown into the deep end in more ways than one. Still, I was not convinced that I wanted to be a journalist. I did the bare minimum to stay on the "journalism track" while exploring modules in other fields like advertising and research. On hindsight, this helped broaden my perspectives. My final-year project, for instance, was an advertising campaign.

Editor's Note: Walter may have wandered far, exploring other areas beyond his chosen specialisation but that didn't stop him from topping his class among those who opted to focus in journalism.

Next, let's get a sense of your "beyond classroom" learning as an undergraduate. You were part of a team behind a nation-wide advertising campaign to promote work-life balance, working with organisations like Health Promotion Board and Tiger Balm. In terms of editorial internships, you were with two vastly different outfits – IS Magazine and Reuters News. Can you give us a sense of your approach towards Practice Learning and how it opened doors for you?

I strongly believe that classroom theory is no substitute for the experience of hands-on learning. Just take a topical example. For all the hype about online tours that travel agencies have rolled out during the Covid-19 pandemic, they – to me – are definitely not a substitute for the real experience of being a tourist, physically present to explore the nooks and crannies of fascinating destinations.

As an undergraduate, I sought out an unpaid internship at I-S magazine. That was my first brush with newsroom journalism. Joining a small outfit helped a lot because I was assigned cover stories from the get-go. Working in a small team also meant there was no hierarchy, making it easy to bounce ideas off the supervisors. It was here that I learnt how to liaise with newsmakers and those in public relations.

Reuters, where I did my official internship, was key in honing my news sense on global news. I recall the buzz in its Asia HQ newsroom as images of the 11 March 2011 tsunami started to come in. Later on, the Singapore bureau gave me my first foray into political reporting at GE2011. I also learnt about business reporting, starting from scratch as I familiarized myself with, among other things, bread and butter stuff like company profit-and-loss statements and balance sheets.

Through an advertising campaign which I worked on with Tiger Balm and the Health Promotion Board, I learnt how to be a more well-rounded thinker. In this case, being on the "other side" of the journalism/marketing divide and yet having journalistic experience helped. I could zoom in on what would make a campaign relevant to potential sponsors and media outlets to pitch it accordingly.

Looking back, the big picture for me is this: Way before today's talk of the need for undergraduates to be versatile and to embrace multi-disciplinary learning, I was fortunate to be in an environment where people enjoyed exploring new things – often purely out of personal interest, without too much thought of the practical gains. We did all kinds of things and learnt to, as Steve Jobs would put it in an iconic commencement speech at Stanford, "connect the dots". Clearly, his exposure to calligraphy, with details like serif and sans seri typefaces, was somewhat accidental and not in line with his technical background. Yet that which was a "distraction" later proved pivotal when he was involved in designing the first Macintosh computer.

After graduation in 2012, you joined The Straits Times, starting out at News Desk. An SPH write up on its correspondents describes your early days there thus: "At The Straits Times, (Walter) first cut his teeth on the crime desk, covering everything from lurid sex-for-corruption trials and murders to the Little India riot in 2013." You then moved to the Political Desk where you "reported on the death of founding prime minister Lee Kuan Yew and was in the thick

of the action of Singapore's General Election in 2015." According to the write up mentioned, you count among the highlights of your career "the chance to interview former President S R Nathan one-on-one for three different stories." **Overall, can you share more about your first few years at SPH before your move to Tokyo? Looking back, what would you consider the most important learning points for someone starting out in his or her career?**

One recent realisation I've had is that I've spent more time as a reporter in Tokyo than as a reporter in Singapore! Looking back at my first few years in SPH, I think I was very fortunate to have been given a range of opportunities that cut across different desks. I benefited from having very good mentors and supervisors who were willing to listen to ideas and to explore different story angles. Part of all this had to do with being at the right place at the right time. While I was on the crime desk, there were several Page One-worthy, high-profile corruption cases as well as the Little India riot. This significantly raised my profile among the editors, which positioned me for a move to the political desk in time for the 2015 General Election.

Looking back, I think there are a few important learning points for someone starting out. One, always ask and clarify anything that is unclear. Two, do not see inexperience as a liability. Rather, view it as a chance to pitch daring new ideas or suggest things that can be done differently. Of course, one must at the same time read the room, so to speak, so as not to step on toes unnecessarily. Three, actively pound the ground and do good old-fashioned legwork so as to build up contacts. Social media is also a good breeding ground to identify new trends. Finally, do not rely solely on one source. Instead always triangulate everything one sees and hears.

In June 2016, you started a new chapter with your move to Japan as foreign correspondent. I understand that you fell in love with the country and decided to pick up Japanese following your first trip there – a solo adventure to Tokyo – in 2012. **Can you say more about your interest in Japan and how you became a foreign correspondent there? More importantly, what enabled you to turn aspiration into reality?**

Japan, as those who have been there know, is an incredibly vibrant place with too much to see, do, eat and discover. My solo trip to Tokyo – a belated graduation gift to myself – did not consciously shape my mind to one day become a Japan correspondent. It was simply my first exposure to the country's culture, hospitality, sights and sounds. And it ended with me wanting to return again someday – at least for another holiday. I did the trip in late 2012, about half a year after I started work.

Cliched as it may sound, when 2013 came along, I then decided to pick up Japanese as a convenient New Year's resolution. Hence I began my weekly classes at a Japanese language school in Singapore. I had no prior background in the language. These weekly classes continued for a while. What then happened was a confluence of factors, which I suppose reinforces how being at the right place at the right time is crucial.

As mentioned earlier, I was on the Political Desk during GE 2015. One day, I was asked to cover a weekend community event that even the editors said was unlikely to yield any story. Feeling more than a little burnt out after working consecutive days, I negotiated for an afternoon off so that I could attend my Japanese class. In exchange, I would cover another event. That was the first time my editors – out of interest – found out that I was studying Japanese. After the GE, I somehow felt I had experienced enough of being a reporter in Singapore and was contemplating a job switch.

At that time, ST was recalibrating its editorial priorities and expanding its overseas coverage. The Japan bureau had been defunct for a couple of years. The previous bureau chief retired while a replacement had not worked out. So the editors were looking to fill the role again. This was especially as Japan began to regain its global prominence under then-PM Shinzo Abe. While the editors had interviewed a couple of other people, things did not work out. Then my supervisor told them that I was studying Japanese. Everything then happened very quickly. I was asked if I wanted the chance to work as a reporter in Japan. My answer was of course Yes. So I moved to Foreign Desk for an introductory stint while settling the necessary administrative work for the move.

As a foreign correspondent, you report on Japan-related stories, features and analyses and have covered domestic politics (e.g. national elections and imperial succession), trade and economics, foreign policy and social issues like ageing and climate change. Broadly, can you share about some of the thrills and challenges you've experienced in your move from Singapore to Tokyo?

The thrills really come from having a ringside seat in a dynamic society that is at odds with modernity and tradition. It is also exciting to find a new rhythm to life in an entirely different country and to practise my Japanese while making mistakes along the way. As a bonus, there is the joy of travelling and finding places off the beaten track. The way many things are done in Japan will bewilder any fresh-eyed Singaporean – and that was me at first. Indeed, the dissonance was especially great in my first few months. It is once again amplified during the Covid-19 pandemic when I have been stupefied by many things. This is Japan, the land of high tech gadgets, and yet we have practical issues like its inability to use technology for contact-tracing and its need to have vaccination records that are paper-based. Things can get puzzling, to say the least.

More broadly, most of the struggles for me had come from being in Japan alone. There was no one to assist me in any sort of handover since I had moved in to fill an empty position. I barely had any help with local administrative matters such as opening a bank account or setting up a mobile phone line. And then there was the annoying matter of how, when I started here, many government agencies require RSVP for events to be returned by fax. Not knowing anyone meant I had to actively try to make friends – which was a bit of a struggle primarily because of my personality. I tend to find socialising exhausting, though I can switch on the "network mode" for purposes of work. Plus, the challenges also stem from how I did not have any immediate predecessors from whom to inherit a bunch of ready contacts. This also meant having to make a lot of cold calls especially at first.

Furthermore, there was the issue of language. Business Japanese is entirely different from the conversational Japanese used in day-to-day interactions. Then there was also the issue of business etiquette like how emails are written, how name cards are exchanged (with both hands), how far to bow in greeting, how formal a greeting should be and so on. Even today, I don't think I've fully grasped all these complexities.

Still on the topic of your move to Tokyo, what have been some of the major adjustments needed on your part, both professionally and personally? What personal traits and background have come in handy to help you cope as a foreign correspondent?

Working alone also took some getting used to, especially with the incessant changes going on at SPH. In my years here, I've gone through different Foreign Editors, each with distinctive demands and workstyles. Trying to manage expectations as to what is reasonably doable can be a chore on its own. As a one-man operation, I take my own photos and produce my own videos for my long-form features – above and beyond the reporting. All this takes a considerable amount of time on top of the bread-and-butter that is breaking news.

I would like to believe my formative years have helped me to be independent and resourceful. So, in a sink-or-swim situation, I will most certainly find ways to survive. On the other hand, I'm prone to second-guessing myself and there is somewhat a sense of the imposter syndrome. Am I too young and inexperienced to be entrusted a role like this? Are my stories good enough? Am I approaching stories correctly? To overcome that, I worked doubly hard especially in my first year or so here. All this has helped me grow in confidence in my stories as I continually work towards covering Japan as widely and as deeply as possible. Having been thrown into the deep end and survived, I feel I have become more resilient. Over the years, I've also come to appreciate the trust that my editors have in me to deliver.

In your job, you need, as you yourself have noted, "a nose for news, an eye for detail and an interest in building relationships". In essence, a lot of what

you do calls for curiosity and networking – traits that are highly valued but often lacking. **Taking some of the recent features you have done, can you give us a glimpse of how you work which has enabled you to unearth interesting stories, with all their colourful details?**

Editor's Note: In a feature, Walter offers insights into the plight of descendants of the burakumin *in Japan – the underclass in a centuries-old social hierarchy who were deemed "unclean" because their jobs often involved animals, blood or death. In yet another feature, he tackles the well known issue of Japan's struggle with suicide, offering details like its notorious "suicide forest" of Aokigahara, the scandal surrounding a serial killer who used Twitter to lure victims, and the country's appointment of "Minister of Loneliness".*

I think curiosity is one of the most important traits anyone, especially young journalists, should have. Rather than take things at face value, one should peel beneath the surface to look at reasons why things are the way they are. It is also essential to keep an open mind, especially when covering a country that appears to be homogeneous but is, in reality, diverse and culturally rich.

I approach my task in a few ways. One, read and understand a wide range of sources. The concerns of those who live in Tokyo will be very different from, say, those who live in Fukushima. For instance, in Tokyo, Covid-19 led to real anxieties over the 2020 Olympic Games. It was very easy for people overseas or in other areas of Japan to say they wanted the Games to happen when they did not have to suffer the consequences. In Fukushima, there are continuing concerns over the nuclear cleanup, including the plan to release tritiated water into the Pacific, as well as rejuvenation of towns that were once under exclusion zones. Two, tap resources such as the Library at the Foreign Correspondents' Club of Japan (FCCJ). The Library is a great help especially when I want to access stories in regional newspapers. It can also help me to locate contacts.

Three, monitor the news, both on television and print media. I get Twitter alerts whenever prominent media tweet new headlines while my daily media monitoring involves reading headlines on NHK, Nikkei, Asahi,

Mainichi, Sankei, Yomiuri, Kyodo, Jiji Press and Japan Times. I need to be aware of each publication's orientation. For instance, there is a difference in the political bent of Asahi, which is liberal, compared to Yomiuri, which is conservative. So they may approach the same story via different angles. Knowing this and being exposed to the differences helps me to frame a more balanced approach towards stories. Four, I watch variety television shows to unwind but they actually also provide deep insights into what is trending in society and what makes it tick. Five, I keep up with trends on Twitter, the most popular social media platform in Japan. Six, I listen to podcasts. Though this is still a nascent medium in Japan, I'm a regular listener of a podcast called History Of Japan by a Hokkaido-based American historian. He provides deep glimpses into Japanese society from prehistoric times to contemporary history.

Politics, diplomacy and defence issues are understandably the bread-and-butter of my coverage. But I frankly think the most interesting stories are those that cover the social aspects of everyday life that not many people abroad may know about. Through such stories, they can get a glimpse of what makes Japanese society tick. The Twitter killer story you refer to, by itself, was dramatic enough to capture attention. But I felt it was important to go beyond the "wire agency" approach of telling the story to give a wider picture of how the horrific killings had happened by exploring the broader social aspects. I guess my experience on the Crime desk helped tremendously in my approach to this story. As for the burakumin feature, it was heartening for me that it was very well read and received positive feedback even from Japanese readers. All this goes beyond the writer and the writing. The point is to raise issues and, in this case, we were dealing with a very real and poignant one which society has tried to bury for far too long.

The SPH write up has described you further this way: "When he's not writing, he loves cafe hopping and exploring new places. He is part of the generation who inexplicably feels the need to capture on Instagram almost everything pretty." Picking up the point about exploring new places in particular, I note

that you, though based in Tokyo, have reported extensively from places like Hokkaido, Fukushima, Kobe and Hiroshima. Regarding the different Japanese cities mentioned, what – for you – uniquely comes to mind for each of them?

Japan comprises 47 prefectures, all of which are individually larger in size than Singapore. It is a fallacy to equate Japan to Tokyo. Every region has its own characteristics, heritage, food, dialect, culture and even local government. This also gives rise to very different issues in different prefectures and cities. Here is a sampling of localised issues and what makes each of them unique. Hokkaido, known for its intensely cold winters, deals with several clear issues. In terms of heritage, the Ainu were deprived of government recognition of their indigeneous status until very recently. Then we have the territorial disputes with Russia over the Northern Territories. Also an issue is tourism, with the town of Niseko (where many Singaporean developers are building property) struggling in the recent winter due to Covid-19 curbs.

Fukushima still grapples with issues surrounding the nuclear cleanup and decommissioning of the Fukushima Daiichi nuclear power plant. Adding to concerns among local fishermen is the planned release of tritiated water into the Pacific Ocean. Kyoto, as Japan's ancient capital, is perhaps known for its centuries-old businesses, shrines and temples. But these have come under strain as a younger generation is shying away from traditional businesses. Hiroshima and Nagasaki are the world's only two cities to suffer from the horrors of atomic bombings.

Okinawa was the last prefecture to return to Japan after WWII and is home to many US army bases whose presence continues to rankle locals. Interesting nugget: Because of its US influence, Okinawa is the only prefecture in Japan where A&W restaurants can be found. Yokohama, in Kanagawa prefecture south of Tokyo, has been in the news in part because of the city's bid to host an Integrated Resort. So a city mayor election here, which ordinarily won't be news, would take on significance as the poll may well become a referendum on the bid.

Niigata, on the Sea of Japan/East Sea coast, meanwhile, is where the majority of the North Korean abductees hail from. Kamikatsu, a small town in Tokushima, was the first in Japan to set a zero-waste goal. One can cite countless other examples but the broader point is clear – the complexity of places is amazing and the learning never stops for the curious minded.

Editor's Note: *For a glimpse of Walter's adventures discovering the diversity of Japan, here is what he has penned in a column for The Straits Times. "The most avid travellers among foreign residents in Japan – myself included – have a bucket list to visit all 47 of the country's prefectures at least once. Having lived in Japan for over five years and visited the country numerous times prior to that, I am now five short of hitting that goal. However, not too many of my Japanese friends seem to share this enthusiasm to explore their backyard, citing such reasons as being too bogged down by work, a lack of time, or an even bigger interest in overseas travel. I personally see the appeal of discovering the je ne sais quoi in each region – that indescribable local vibe nurtured through centuries of heritage and culture – which differentiates, say, rural Aomori in the north-east from Ehime in the west, or even between Tokyo and Osaka."*

In 2018, you also visited North Korea for a six-day reporting trip. This must have been eye-opening. What stood out for you?

On North Korea, what really stood out for me was the sense of an alternate reality among the locals, inbred with the Juche mindset that is both superior and yet reluctantly reliant on the free world. Our minders, perhaps wanting to impress, treated us to sumptuous meals that were impossible to finish. I felt bad given the extreme poverty that exists outside of Pyongyang (a topic which they try to avoid). The minders also freely admitted to watching Chinese dramas on their locally-made smartphones, which were equipped with games akin to Angry Birds. They were very friendly to us, perhaps owing to the goodwill from the Trump-Kim summit that year.

Yet they were stubbornly insistent when asked difficult questions like how their hoped-for reunification with South Korea will look like given the vast ideological differences between the two countries. Will South Koreans adopt communism and see Kim Jong Un as their leader? Will North Korea be comfortable with the "one country, two systems" model given the vast economic differences between the two Koreas? Will South Korean youth, already poverty-stricken, be willing to fund their neighbours to the North? These are all complex questions. A short trip alone can already yield all kinds of questions and raise all sorts of issues.

Finally, Walter, let's end on a broad note. With the benefit of having a ringside seat based in one of the world's most vibrant and fascinating yet arguably little understood countries, how important has curiosity been to help you do a good job? Broadening somewhat, what would you tell the young about this trait – and others like it such as resilience, versatility and "can-doism" – as they prepare themselves for the demands of today's volatile workplace?

I cannot over emphasize the importance of being curious, of being open to new ideas and perspectives. For youth who are preparing to enter today's volatile workplace, being curious will give them an edge especially if they can approach conventional issues differently and if they are willing to step out of their comfort zones.

LOVE FOR WORDS

Picture courtesy of Walter Sim

"Socially, I was incredibly awkward as a child – to the point where I struggled to fit in with my peers despite attending traditionally good schools.....As an only child whose parents were somewhat distant and left me to my own devices, I was quite withdrawn and this could have added to my lack of confidence. But this played a part in honing my interest in reading and, by extension, global affairs. I remember spending a lot of time reading. I could recite world capitals when I was very young and would occasionally even peruse the encyclopedia. This love for words also extended to reading The Straits Times everyday as my family had a subscription....(Later in university), I benefited from a six-month student exchange programme at the Jonkoping University in Sweden in 2009. There were some special moments. For example, as part of a course I took, I produced a live TV segment that went on air on local television. Until then I never really did have the chance to go abroad (my parents don't really like the hassle of air travel). So the exchange experience was invaluable for me to broaden my worldview. I took the chance to explore Europe widely, learning about European history and cultures. I also made some friends along the way. Having tasted the value of an exchange, I followed up on that by looking out for overseas immersion programmes (including one in Vietnam)."

—*Walter Sim*

MYSTICAL MUSINGS

"As the second world war was breaking out, Henry Miller visited Greece at the invitation of his friend Lawrence Durrell and travelled around it for several months. The result was The Colossus of Maroussi, *at once a love letter to a great world civilisation and a poetic expression of Miller's mystical musings. There is little in the way of traditional 'travel' here: the sights, smells and sounds are present only inasmuch as they trigger feelings and emotions. This book taught me that real travel writing must involve an 'inner' element, either by detailing an inner journey or by creating a resonance to which the reader can respond. Take that away and you're left with either reportage or a guidebook."*

JASON WEBSTER ON *THE COLOSSUS OF MAROUSSI* BY HENRY MILLER

Source: The Guardian

EXPLAINING NUANCES

Picture courtesy of Balli Kaur

"From a young age, I needed narratives to explain the complexities of my background. I am Singaporean but from the Punjabi Sikh community. People I met did not always know that Singapore is multicultural. They thought of Singapore as being somewhere in China or even as a Chinese country (whatever that meant to them). So, with the way I looked and all, I did not really fit into their preconceptions. Similar explanations about my background seemed to be necessary no matter where we lived. This was despite the fact that we were always in international communities, enclaves really, and I went to international, America-centric schools. Although the students and teachers came from all over the world, the prevailing ethos in these schools – unfortunately though inevitably then – was that the American way was the best. That created a strange consistency despite the transience of my circumstances. But it didn't resolve the issue of my identity – for me and for those around me........Then, whenever we came back to Singapore from a posting abroad, I had to justify my claim about being Singaporean just because I had been living in Russia or Japan, for example. On top of that, as a Punjabi Sikh, I am from a small minority within a minority group in Singapore, so I did not attend Tamil classes or celebrate Deepavali. These nuances also needed to be explained."

—Balli Kaur

CHAPTER 6

Citizen of the World

Balli Kaur Jaswal
Author & Lecturer

By Ulrike Murfett & CCJ

Pictures courtesy of Balli Kaur

Balli, born in Singapore, you grew up all over the world and have lived in countries like Japan, Russia, Turkey, the United States, Australia and the Philippines. Generally, how has being a "citizen of the world", so to speak, shaped you as an individual and how does that translate to you being the writer that you are today?

I had an unusual childhood. My father worked for the Singapore Foreign Ministry, which meant that we lived in many different countries and cultures. This has certainly shaped my identity. Moving around so much, I was always on the outside, never truly belonging. This may cause some disorientation and can prove challenging for someone young in particular. But it also meant I developed a strong inner world and books and stories provided consistency. I could hold onto the narratives I created, even if everything else in my world was changing.

From a young age, I needed narratives to explain the complexities of my background. I am Singaporean but from the Punjabi Sikh community. People I met did not always know that Singapore is multicultural. They thought of Singapore as being somewhere in China or even as a Chinese country (whatever that meant to them). So, with the way I looked and all, I did not really fit into their preconceptions. Similar explanations about my background seemed to be necessary no matter where we lived. This was despite the fact that we were always in international communities, enclaves really, and I went to international, America-centric schools. Although the students and teachers came from all over the world, the prevailing ethos in these schools – unfortunately though inevitably then – was that the American way was the best. That created a strange consistency despite the transience of my circumstances. But it didn't resolve the issue of my identity – for me and for those around me.

Then, whenever we came back to Singapore from a posting abroad, I had to justify my claim about being Singaporean just because I had been living in Russia or Japan, for example. On top of that, as a Punjabi Sikh, I am from a small minority within a minority group in Singapore, so I did not attend Tamil classes or celebrate Deepavali. These nuances also needed to be explained. Responding to questions about my identity necessitated stories that helped to illustrate who I was (and am), and that was probably good training for a writer.

I think my experiences abroad have pulled me out of my shell. I am an introvert, a homebody by nature. But I became more extroverted simply because I had to assert myself to provide these explanations about who I was. It has also been instructive to observe the reactions I have got regarding descriptions related to the complexities and transience in my life. I've lived abroad both as a child and as an adult. From my observations, I would say that kids seem to be more accepting of the unusual. They might have been puzzled that I did not look Japanese although I said I lived in Japan. But they were content with the explanation that my father's job meant we were living there. Adults, on the other hand, might react in two very different ways. Those with exposure to similar experiences tend to understand quickly whereas others find my background "just too complicated", perhaps because I do not easily fit into their frames of reference.

In an interview with Helmi Yusof (The Business Times, 27 June 2019), who memorably described you as "the most internationally well-known Singapore novelist after *Crazy Rich Asians*' Kevin Kwan", you said, "When you're moving from place to place and you have to deal with culture shock and feeling lonely and anxious about fitting in, it's very reassuring to have books to escape into. The characters are always there and things always work out in the end." What books – in terms of genres and specific authors or titles – were you into which served the purpose you have mentioned? What other avenues did you have in terms of escapism growing up in different cultures?

The first books I read were very American and very "white", simply because of the type of schools I went to. There wasn't much diversity in what I read. But a shift in the publishing world occurred in the mid-nineties which correlated with a shift in my understanding of who I wanted to be and what I wanted to do. I became acquainted with female authors from India and the diaspora whose work had been picked up by publishing giants of the

West and thus became available in big bookstores. Global interest in good and intriguing stories, also from this part of the world, had diminished the need for a western context.

Arundhati Roy's book *The God of Small Things* was read widely in the Indian diaspora and generated a lot of pride. I did not understand the book initially but was delighted that someone like me could write like that. Later, when I reread it with more maturity, I understood what she was doing and realised what an incredible book this was – and still is. It showed me there was space for my stories, even if I did not have blonde hair and blue eyes. But it wasn't just books that provided an escape route for me. I also liked writing and music. We all loved the radio deejays!

Editor's Note: Kaur's reference to Arundhati Roy is instructive. The winner of the acclaimed Booker Prize in 1997 for The God of Small Things, Roy is among a host of Indian writers leading the way in what Deccan Herald terms "one of the most landmark accomplishments of the Indian literary firmament in recent decades." She and writers like Amitav Ghosh, Tarun Tejpal and Kiran Desai have found widespread followings outside their own country, and been translated into other languages with remarkable success. Take, for instance, The God of Small Things. A story set against the backdrop of social discrimination, communism and the caste system, it has been compared favorably to the works of Faulkner and Dickens. Publisher Penguin Random House puts it this way: "Arundhati Roy's modern classic is equal parts powerful family saga, forbidden love story, and piercing political drama....Lush, lyrical, and unnerving, (the novel) is an award-winning landmark that started for its author an esteemed career of fiction and political commentary that continues unabated."

Although you lived out of the country because of your father's work with the Ministry of Foreign Affairs, you were born in Singapore and studied here between the ages of eight and 15. While here, your experiences with books were rather mixed, with teachers worried about the influence of the Sweet Valley High teen romances which appealed to you and your classmates, for

instance. **Can you say more about such experiences which, on hindsight, might seem rather amusing?**

My teachers categorised books into "good" or "bad", which appeared to me very judgmental and moralistic. Dating and romance were taboo topics and our teachers were alarmed about western influence in the books that we liked to read. As a child, I felt ashamed about enjoying books that were meant for enjoyment and felt guilty, like I was leading everyone astray. Perhaps my background of going to international schools where topics were discussed more liberally was interpreted as dangerous by some of my teachers here.

Thinking about this now as an adult, I do not find it (the disapproval) amusing but I can recognise how ridiculous these teachers were (whatever their good intentions) and perhaps even laugh about it, which I couldn't as a child. Interestingly, in my brother's all-boys school, books that contained violence, for example, were not similarly censured. There was clearly a very gendered approach to books and reading. But even then, there were authors who exerted a huge influence on me. Take Judy Blume, for instance. To me then, she understood the experience of being young and was never condescending or patronising. She spoke the truth to us kids and that was powerful. I wanted to achieve this in my writing as well.

Today, you are the author of several books. First a pointed observation – that in itself is quite a feat in Singapore's context, given our famous pragmatism. Broadly, what would you say are the confluence of factors that have enabled you to publish several books?

Being shamed in school for enjoying certain books and writing so much and being told that it wasn't a very pragmatic pursuit by parents and relatives – all that made me even more determined to continue with it. When I was 18, I was ready to spread my wings, but did not really know what I wanted to do. But I had the great good luck to attend a small women-only liberal arts college in Virginia and it changed my life. Remarkably, this college had an incredible creative writing programme, supportive yet challenging, and it taught me so much. To this day I am not sure if I could tap into my creativity had it not been for the years I spent there. Now I write every day, even if it is only half an hour or even less. Slow and steady wins the race! This requires some discipline, because I am not a very patient person, but I try to keep focused on what I want the end product to be.

Next, beyond simply producing the works, what stands out in your case is the success (for want of a better term) you have enjoyed. For instance, you were named Best Young Australian Novelist of 2014 by the Sydney Morning Herald following your first novel, *Inheritance*. Your second novel, *Sugarbread*, was nominated for the 2015 Epigram Books Fiction Prize. Your bestselling novels have won both critical and commercial acclaim around the world. But you also do not want to be "pigeon-holed" as a writer of just the Punjabi diaspora and so would like your next novel to feature Filipino domestic workers in Singapore. What do you think accounts for the appeal of your works?

I did not really think that there would be much interest in stories that focus on the marginalised, because we do not hear such narratives all that often. It appears that I was wrong and my readers find these stories as fascinating as I do. Writing about the marginalised is indeed very important to me. But when I started out, the interest of the publishing world in such stories was still quite limited. Publishers weren't keen on more complicated narratives, like an East-West conflict might entail. For example, I was told that *Inheritance*, which came out in 2013, was just too unfamiliar. In many people's minds, Singapore was still associated with being Chinese and a story about a Punjabi Sikh family migrating to Singapore required perhaps too big a leap from readers. Even now, a debut author might find it difficult to get a story like *Inheritance* published. Indian people settling in Singapore still confounds readers, unlike Indian people settling in Britain.

In recent years, however, the attention paid to authors of colour, to diversity and fiction from around the world has grown tremendously. Where there was room for only one diaspora writer and one story per year, there are now much wider, more nuanced interests. This is a development that has clearly benefitted me and the stories I want to tell. I think it is important to make stories appealing to readers. For example, the title *Erotic Stories for Punjabi Widows* already implies some entertainment, but there are also deeper, darker themes of domestic violence and other shadows that have fallen onto the community. I would be doing a disservice to the characters and the community I am writing about, if I only mention the good without the bad or vice versa.

I have been accused of portraying the Punjabi community in a negative light, but this is not what my books are about. Instead, in my books, I have tried to make sense of immigrant experiences. How, for example, do progressive young Indians in the diaspora navigate the confusion of growing up in conservative families still tethered to their country of origin? But I do not want to be labelled as "the writer of Punjabi novels." As you mentioned, my new book is set in Singapore and focuses on the life of Filipina domestic helpers. I think the literary scene in Singapore welcomes the voices of minority communities. My two first novels, *Inheritance* and *Sugarbread*, were well received by Indian, Chinese and Malay readers.

Akshita Nanda, writing for The Straits Times in 2017, described your novels – which address "complex issues, from race relations to living with schizophrenia" – as "both enjoyable and intelligent." This mix of enjoyment and intelligence – where does that come from? Can you give us a glimpse of your writing style which has both depth and reach? What facilitates this effect?

Editor's Note: Inheritance, for instance, tackles mental health issues and the dysfunctional dynamics in a Punjabi family in Singapore. Sugarbread tackles the issue of racism in Singapore through the perspective of a young narrator.

In my books, I try to infuse themes of social justice with humour, heart, smart dialogues and characterisations to give them intelligence and depth while retaining their accessibility to the readers. When I write, I consider how I would like the story to be told. How much darkness and negativity do I want my readers to be exposed to? Would I prefer joy and humour to be in the mix as well? This makes it easier to strike that balance between depth and reach.

If you are too immersed in the idea of writing well-crafted sentences and creating multidimensional characters, your work can feel quite insular. It is in your head only and not going anywhere. But I try to work on stuff like sentences and characterisations by thinking more about movement. Where is the story heading, how does the character grow? My writing style has evolved together with my experiences. *Inheritance* was very character driven. I really wanted to get to know the characters and did not think so much about the experience I as a reader would want. My later novels are more plot driven and have larger casts interacting with each other.

It's known that you are committed to writing "1,000 words a day, regardless of quality". Broadly, can we get a glimpse of your writing process as a novelist?

We need an update on what is written about me. When I was writing the *Shergill Sisters,* I had a deadline with Harper Collins, had just started my PhD and was pregnant with my son. All this imposed a literal deadline on me. I did not have the time to sit around and ponder. The "1000 words a day" commitment helped me to meet deadlines. I do not necessarily write like that anymore, especially because now I need to balance writing and teaching. I find that I'm a bit more productive in writing when I have the stress of other things that need to be done as well. In contrast, when I was working on *Shergill Sisters*, my whole day revolved around getting the story down which, in a way, was harder. Right now, I am not being held to any major deadline, so I try to set myself less precise goals. For example, how much should I get done by the end of the month?

Interestingly, *Erotic Stories for Punjabi Widows* and *The Unlikely Adventures of the Shergill Sisters* are being adapted for the screen. To me, this is a positive development – an opportunity, I guess, for your works to reach more people. For you, what is exciting about the transition from print to screen? What are some concerns you have and how do you get round them?

When a story transitions from print to screen, I'd like to see the essence of the story preserved. Understandably, I will hope that the experience readers get from the story isn't compromised. Of course, some major parts of the plot will change. This is because not everything can easily be translated into film and there is only so much that can be done in 90 minutes to capture the audience's attention. But the viewers must still get an understanding of the story's characters, their world and their journey. This is the essence which must be preserved.

Erotic Stories for Punjabi Widows generated a lot of interest from film producers from the time of its publication. I made it a point to be involved in the discussions with producers. Why? I worried about stereotyping and negative impact. If a book about a small migrant community is being published in the West, where there is a particular narrative about migrant communities and there isn't much space in the media for appropriate representations, things can go haywire.

Thankfully, Scott Free, the production company that took on *Erotic Stories*, was adamant from the start that they did not want a "white gaze" film. This was a powerful and reassuring statement to make. They also discussed changes in the industry and what they had learned from them, which I found fascinating. They have been genuinely interested in preserving the story, keeping it authentic, shying away from stereotypes and being careful about representation. All this has given me the sense that there is an opportunity for the film to do justice to the book. *Shergill Sisters* is being adapted for a television series. This is a little different from *Erotic Stories*, which is being adapted for a feature film. I've also been quite involved in this process and my thoughts are valued by the team, which is great.

Talking further about reach, Hollywood star Reese Witherspoon picked *Erotic Stories for Punjabi Widows* for her online book club – a move which sent sales soaring in the US, India and Singapore. It is also heartening to note too that translation rights for the novel have been sold in countries like France, Spain,

Italy, Poland, Israel, Greece, Sweden and Brazil. Did these developments surprise you and how did you react to them?

Yes, Reese Witherspoon choosing the book was a complete surprise and really changed the book's visibility. A book by a Singaporean author about Punjabi widows in England is perhaps unlikely to become mainstream reading in the US, but it did because of her. She made the effort to look at those untold stories and to take a chance on this book by a new author she had not heard of. The book has also created interest in surprisingly diverse markets. I think the first translation right was sold in Estonia, then in Sweden, Poland, Germany, Russia, and Spain, which has been very exciting. But I do ask myself how a book like this will be received in languages or cultures I do not know much about and what, if any, impressions of the Punjabi community already exist there.

I do not have much to do with the translation process, because I do not work with the translators or the editors. I do see the final product but I cannot read it! Perhaps I should get someone to read the Bulgarian edition, for example. That edition is twice as thick as the English version and full of footnotes, which is something I very much avoid in my own writing, but which might be the style of the publisher. Or this – the need for more detailed explanations via footnotes – is just necessary for that culture.

I also have an update on the Chinese translation. The book will not be available in the Chinese market after all. There was a lot of interest in translating the book and then, a year later, my agent was told that some changes would be needed to get the book through the Chinese censorship process. I was not privy to these conversations. But in early 2020, I received a letter from the Chinese government saying this book had not passed inspection and would not be translated because of the sexuality it contains. Unfortunately, that was the end of the Chinese venture.

Beyond literature, you have also ventured into other forms of writing. For instance, your essays and op-eds about diaspora, migrant identities,

censorship, racism and sexuality have been published in the New York Times, South China Morning Post, Harper's Bazaar India, Conde Nast Traveller, Griffith Review and other publications. **How does this – the move into popular writing – complement your primary identity as a creative writer?**

My writing of op eds and essays started as part of the publicity initiatives for my novels, *Erotic Stories* and *Shergill Sisters*. Publishers develop a marketing strategy and my publicist discusses with me the topics that might interest me and be in line with the focus of the books. This is an opportunity to publicise the books because their themes connect to these topics. I like it, because I get to talk about those topics directly to the audience in the straight-forward way of non-fiction. For example, I wrote something about female foeticide, a topic with comes up in one of my novels. It is a fascinating topic, but I cannot put a lot of research and my own opinion into the novel unless it is woven into the narrative. Writing op eds is a nice way of making my views known.

Editor's Note: For a flavour of Kaur's op eds, consider this piece for The South China Morning Post written in 2019 which is a call for an honest discussion about prejudice in the wake of controversy in Singapore over a brownface ad and a provocative rap video. Kaur writes: "The race riots: Singapore's biggest bogeyman. Growing up, we were taught that the island state's success depended on peace between ethnic groups. From race-based housing quotas to prevent ghettoisation to annual Racial Harmony Day celebrations in schools, the government promotes the coexistence of Chinese, Malays, Indians and Others (this is an official category). If you believe the rhetoric about slippery slopes, we are always one malicious tweet away from descending into chaos."

Outside of writing, you have also conducted workshops at international writers' festivals on topics like creative writing, global citizenship and the use of literature as a medium for social justice advocacy. Can you say more about these training opportunities? Overall, how do you view your different pursuits – eg creative writing, writing for media, advocacy – and what do they say about what you stand for?

I have held creative writing workshops on a range of topics both locally and overseas at writers' festivals. I focus on generic creative writing skills like characterisations and settings or on topics I like to write about. I've also given keynote addresses on the power of storytelling and, as you mentioned, global citizenship or social justice advocacy in literature. These are topics I can draw on from personal experience. I make sure people understand that I am no expert, that I offer personal experience and my observations as an author.

All my different pursuits – the creative writing, the writing for media, the advocacy – are building blocks of my identity. It is a privilege to be able to write novels that tell stories about that identity and about other people discovering more about aspects of their own identity. I am very curious and ask lots of questions. I think that's what I love about writing; it is an exercise in perpetual curiosity. There is nothing that I enjoy more than helping to shape a work of writing or shaping my own. Running a workshop, for example, and seeing how ideas come together can be satisfying. A writer figuring out how exactly a work can be stronger, how the atmosphere can be richer, what works and what doesn't work – all that is fascinating to me. It all adds to my desire to follow my curiosities.

A former writer-in-residence at the University of East Anglia, you have a PhD in Creative Writing from the Nanyang Technological University and are currently lecturing at Yale-NUS College. Finally, Balli, for a creative writer, why a PhD? How does teaching go with writing in your case?

I had pragmatic reasons for doing a PhD in creative writing. If you want an academic job, not having a PhD is going to hold you back. When I applied for the PhD, I wanted to move from high school teaching to university teaching. 80% of a PhD in creative writing, at least at NTU, is devoted to creative work and 20% to the exegesis, the reflection and critical analysis of the creative part and its context. At that time, I had started writing the *Shergill Sisters*, which meant I was already writing the creative part of a dissertation. It made sense to get a degree out of it. The part I found most challenging about the PhD was the exegesis. Surprisingly, that was also the part I enjoyed most. It was a style of academic writing that I was not very familiar with and tackling that challenge was quite a milestone for me.

I enjoy new challenges, but they have to be linked to what I already enjoy doing. For example, writing op eds was a completely new learning experience for me and I would love to learn more about writing narrative non-fiction. Exploring new formats and genres of writing is very interesting to me and learning more about things I love is exciting. I do not think I would do well with a new challenge like getting a physics degree. I do not like that kind of challenge.

Teaching is quite complementary to writing and gives me another channel for my creativity. Working with words and helping people to find their voices – that inspires me and gives me energy for my own writing. I enjoy lecturing at university very much and do not want to give it up just yet. But a balance has to be struck. The emotional demands, more than the day-to-day routines of my work, can be quite draining, especially now that I have a small child. At the end of the day, I find that my battery is quite empty. Luckily, I have a very supportive partner which helps a lot. But I am still trying to figure out how to juggle everything I want to do. It's a work in progress.

INTRIGUING STORIES

Picture courtesy of Balli Kaur

"The first books I read were very American and very 'white', simply because of the type of schools I went to. There wasn't much diversity in what I read. But a shift in the publishing world occurred in the mid-nineties which correlated with a shift in my understanding of who I wanted to be and what I wanted to do. I became acquainted with female authors from India and the diaspora whose work had been picked up by publishing giants of the West and thus became available in big bookstores. Global interest in good and intriguing stories, also from this part of the world, had diminished the need for a western context. Arundhati Roy's book The God of Small Things *was read widely in the Indian diaspora and generated a lot of pride. I did not understand the book initially but was delighted that someone like me could write like that. Later, when I reread it with more maturity, I understood what she was doing and realised what an incredible book this was – and still is. It showed me there was space for my stories, even if I did not have blonde hair and blue eyes. But it wasn't just books that provided an escape route for me. I also liked writing and music. We all loved the radio deejays!"*

—Balli Kaur

CLARION CALL

"I started reading Full Tilt *on a grey morning, wearing a grey suit, in a crowd of grey faces on the London Underground. Several Central Line stops later, I'd raced with Dervla Murphy and her bicycle, Rosinante, from Dunkirk to Delhi, and made the decision to quit my career as a lawyer and cycle round the world. Funny, ingenuous, gently erudite and intrepid (she kept a .25 revolver in her saddlebag)* Full Tilt *is the best kind of adventure story, and a clarion call to 'travel for travel's sake'. I realised that you don't need a wealth of knowledge and experience to embark on a journey like this. If you believe human wisdom may be measured by the respect we pay to the unattainable, the mysterious or simply the different, and have a flair for getting on with people, you're ready."*

ROBERT PENN ON *FULL TILT* BY DERVLA MURPHY

Source: The Guardian

PARADISE

Picture courtesy of Edwin Koo

"I asked my wife if she would follow me to Nepal, a faraway place – at least in terms of how different it would be from Singapore. She said yes before asking more questions. Yes, fortunately for me, my wife is a very spontaneous person. She was also tired of her old job as an air stewardess and wanted a break. So we gave ourselves two years. While in Nepal, I focused on the local themes that appealed to me – Maoist insurgency and Tibetan refugees. These were also themes that appealed to international publications, so the stars aligned. Of course, I delved into other projects but, in the end, these were the ones that held my attention. Even till now, I continue to find them intriguing. I also had an opportunity to travel to Pakistan in 2009. It was there that I started what I would consider my most important work to date – Paradise. In essence, it is about a paradisical place called Swat Valley which fell prey to both man-made and natural tragedies."

—Edwin Koo

CHAPTER 7

Inner Voice

Edwin Koo
Documentary Photographer

Pictures courtesy of Edwin Koo

Edwin, first the broad strokes. Among other things, you are known in Singapore's photojournalism circle for your choice of what I would consider among the most difficult countries to tell stories with your pictures. Broadly, can you share more about this specific choice and what does it tell us about you?

I think I will tackle this question in two aspects. The first has got to do with normal aspirations, I guess – and is readily understood in the context of Singapore with our emphasis on "doing well". My choice was guided by my desire as a young person wishing to make a name for myself in my early 30s. More generally, there was the desire to express myself artistically through my choice of personal projects. After leaving my career in SPH, I had wanted to pursue independent documentary photography. Back in 2008, this still seemed like a viable option – magazines and newspapers then had budget for independent story ideas as opposed to commissioned story ideas. Basically, the plan was to pursue long-term projects, make sellable stories midway through, and pad all this with a few commissions from well-known magazines. This plan necessarily took me to interesting and sometimes "difficult" places. So in a way, the path was inevitable. Interesting stories and photos do indeed come from interesting places.

The second part of my answer – regarding why difficult places – involves vocation, a "calling" if you like. My choice of pursuing photography, and more specifically photojournalism, stems from an inner personal voice which seeks fulfilment through visual expressions. The reason why anyone would take on a "personal project" is because it is personal to him or her. It goes way beyond dollars and sense. Following a theme or a project for years takes a certain obsession. It is this very obsession which would help one disregard the fact that time spent may not necessarily convert to income or renumeration. In my case, this has led me to choose "difficult" places simply because they are precisely where I can find the very stories that make me tick.

In many ways, you started conventionally enough. You went to top schools like Dunman High and Hwa Chong JC and was valedictorian when you graduated with First Class Honours from NTU's School of Communication & Information

in 2003. Can you give us a glimpse of your growing up years and how they were, I presume, very typical?

As a young person, I had always been able to "do well" in school. I enjoyed doing well. I enjoyed the idea of getting good results and being ahead of the pack. I recall I bought lots of assessment books with my own savings to improve my scores. I cannot explain why I behaved like this. My parents were average folks. My father was a policeman while my mother was a housewife throughout most of my schooling years. They were not highly educated themselves and never pushed me to do better. I never had tuition for my entire school life. I guess I had a role model in my elder sister who also did well in school on her own. The notion of "doing well" was so simple back then – in the late 90s.

On the flipside, given the less than traditional path you have subsequently taken, was something already brewing during your growing up years – whether consciously or otherwise? If so, looking back, how did you manage whatever conflicts there might be (eg between what would be deemed good for your future and what might interest you more personally when it came to choice of disciplines to pursue, for instance?)

When I started my university education at NTU, I had wanted to make lots of money working in an advertising or PR agency. That was why I went into communications. It was a good deviation from my earlier education which was heavily oriented towards mathematics and the sciences. Yet, it still held a promise of a "good life" – going by conventional definition at least. So yes, I was already thinking of how to "do well" in an alternative way. Back then, it was scholarships and civil service and the usual doctor/lawyer route.

Conflicts? They were always there in my case. When it comes to work, one always looks at the pay and how interesting the work is. Usually they are at odds. The other conflict for me was really parental expectations. When I took on my first job in 2003, my father was rather concerned that I studied so much only to end up taking photographs. It helped that I worked in SPH and my bylines were seen regularly. So my parents were assured for a while. Then when I quit my SPH position in 2008, my father was asking me why I did that – quit a stable and respectable job. And to do what? Leave Singapore to go to a developing country with a newly married wife? I guess the conflicts outside of me made me even more determined to go ahead with my plans. Along the way, while I was in Nepal, I had to deal with another kind of conflict: self-doubt.

Ok, now that we get a bit of the back story, let's look at your career path. You studied communication and did an internship at Reuters. Was there a time when you were moving more in the direction of journalism (rather than photojournalism) or perhaps, even more broadly, other careers which might need less explanation (to other people at least) because they would generate better, more obvious returns?

In university, I took up journalism modules. Suddenly, like some of my peers I would imagine, I wanted to change the world for the better (I still do!). I started to work part-time at newspapers as a rookie reporter during my school holidays. So yes, I was already interested in being a text reporter from the very beginning. Then somewhere along the way, I found a sharper focus. I thought I would do business journalism to "move and shake markets" with my reports. It seemed to pay better than general news and reporting in other beats too. Also at that time, I could see that the editors at newspapers were living large, so I figured pay raises and promotion prospects could well be promising. To cut the long story short, for all my idealism, I obviously wasn't immune to the pressures associated with ideas like prestige, comfort and financial gains.

Then I met my photojournalism professor, Shyam Tekwani, a war photographer who worked extensively in Sri Lanka during the insurgence of the Tamil Tigers. His story led me to imagine that I could also be an intrepid photojournalist. Interestingly, it was my final year project, a book called *Rot Fai* (Rail in Thai) which I did under his supervision, that helped me land my first job at SPH. At the point when I signed my first (and last) work contract, I thought it – the pursuit of what I loved strongly as opposed to something deemed more practical – would be a passing phase. I would "grow up" and look for something with "better prospects". At that point, I thought I should do what my youth afforded me and enjoy the prerogative of someone just starting out. However, the more photographs I took, the more I fell in love with the art of photography. And when you are in love, you no longer think much about bread and butter, or the future!

Next, consider the time you discovered photojournalism. Can you share how it came about? That was some time back but can you recall the remarkable clarity of purpose people say they get once they find something they truly love and want to pursue?

At the end of my five-year stint as a photojournalist at SPH, I must say that I was jaded. On one hand, I was getting the hang of daily jobs and it was no longer as challenging as before. On the other hand, I yearned to be "out there" telling my own stories, not illustrating other people's stories using photography. There were so many interesting things to do with photojournalism out there. I wanted to be on my own two feet, seeing how and where I would stand when pitted against the "rest of the world".

The "moment", or should I say moments, happened shortly after my decision to quit my photojournalist position. At 31, I was at a crossroads – remain in photography or seek better paying jobs elsewhere? I even went for an interview to be a pilot. I did a U-turn in the end. I loved my vocation. But to remain in photography would mean I had to figure out how to make the career even better on my own. That fear, that unknown lying in front of me, and my decision to take a step forward – that was my first moment of clarity. There were other smaller "moments", such as when I got a phone call from London saying that I won the Getty Images Grant. It was mindblowing. Suddenly, I was recognized and I was "doing well". All the while, it was a stab in the dark, a very long shot.

Editor's Note: *In 2009, Edwin was awarded The Getty Images Grant for Editorial Photography, one of international photojournalism's top awards.*

Earlier that year, his work on Pakistan also won a third placing in the UNICEF Photo of the Year.

I would say another "moment of clarity" came in 2011 when I returned to Singapore. Once again, it was adversity that made the resolve clearer than ever. I had returned because my wife was pregnant with our first child. Suddenly, we had to face the bread and butter issues of life again. But being away for 2.5 years had left me with no advantage as a freelancer. My Straits Times days were almost three years ago, and I did not leverage on my social capital upon leaving in 2008. It was a clean slate and I was 33 years old. I had to figure out how to make money from the only real skill I had on my CV – photojournalism.

As I struggled in that first year back, in 2011, Singapore's General Election took place. It was that landmark election. I looked for people to hire me to cover it, but no one wanted me. So I took photos anyway for my personal project – *Notes From A Singapore Son*. The photos received a lot of attention on social media (mainly Facebook back then). Subsequently, I launched my first solo exhibition. I remember people like Chiam See Tong, Nicole Seah and Chen Show Mao came to the opening. It was amazing. And that was also my break – jobs started to come in as I got my "five minutes of fame". But it was also a "moment of clarity" for me. It assured me that if I resolve to "do well" in what I love, it will work out for me in the end, come what may.

To back track a little, in 2008, after five years as a news photographer, you left the newsroom and decided to move to Nepal with your wife. First things first, how did you convince your wife to join you on this journey?

I asked my wife if she would follow me to Nepal, a faraway place – at least in terms of how different it would be from Singapore. She said yes before asking more questions. Yes, fortunately for me, my wife is a very spontaneous person. She was also tired of her old job as an air stewardess and wanted a break. So we gave ourselves two years.

Your wife's blessings given, I am not surprised the 2.5 years in Nepal turned out to be among the most fruitful periods in your career. Can you share some highlights in terms of projects and experiences?

While in Nepal, I focused on the local themes that appealed to me – Maoist insurgency and Tibetan refugees. These were also themes that appealed to international publications, so the stars aligned. Of course, I delved into other projects but, in the end, these were the ones that held my attention. Even till now, I continue to find them intriguing. I also had an opportunity to travel to Pakistan in 2009. It was there that I started what I would consider my most important work to date – *Paradise*. In essence, it is about a paradisical place called Swat Valley which fell prey to both man-made and natural tragedies. For this work, I was fortunate to be awarded the ICON de Martell Cordon Bleu, which funded the publication of my book *Paradise*.

Editor's Note: In 2012, Edwin was awarded the prestigious photography accolade, the ICON de Martell Cordon Bleu, which recognises an individual for an outstanding body of work in his photographic career. The book Paradise is a photographic monograph focusing on the notion of paradise for the people in the Swat Valley of Pakistan. Through the documentation of daily life and extraordinary happenings in Swat, he discovers "the fragility of Man's interpretation of paradise, as well as the resilience of the human spirit in the face of hell-on-earth".

Editor's Note: In terms of his overall experience of being in Nepal and how his brief stint there has shaped him deeply, Edwin once told Vulcan Post in an interview: "Nepal taught me very important lessons about life, and indirectly, about photography. It is one of the poorest countries in the world. Many things we take for granted here in Singapore – clean drinking water, 24-hour power supply, good roads – are unattainable for most Nepalese. Kathmandu is one of the most polluted cities in the world. Despite such circumstances, people are open, honest, and friendly. What they lack in material wealth, they more than make up for it in the human spirit.....Living in adversity changes one's perspective of life. Having a hot shower on a cold winter day was a luxury. Having a plate of home cooked nasi lemak was sheer pleasure. Because my wife and I were living mainly off savings, we watched how we spent. We had meat once or twice a week, because it was much more expensive than vegetables. There were not many shopping places in Kathmandu, but our weekends were no less occupied because there was always a celebration or gathering at a friend's place. Life was far less busy in Nepal, but much more fulfilling, because things that kept us busy were more meaningful. Friends made up a very important part of life in Nepal. Many of them went out of their way to help me, a stranger in their land. And this became my method of getting to my stories and photographs – by making friends along the way. I never hired a translator or a guide – it would have made the process less natural, more contrived."

In 2011, you returned to Singapore. **What prompted you to come back? Why not go further in terms of venturing out – eg by staying put in Nepal and going deeper, so to speak, or perhaps by being based in another developing country? What work did you do during this period back in Singapore to support yourself and your family? To the extent possible, how did you try to stay creative even as you met the demands of clients?**

As I shared earlier, I landed my first break in 2011 after the General Election. Back then, I had corporate clients coming to ask me to shoot their annual reports and calendars in black-and-white. They wanted me to apply my personal signature on their products. But to be honest, this trend lasted less than a year. If I had to be really honest about it, client work is seldom about being "creative". At least not in the conventional sense. Being "creative" means being good at interpreting your client's needs and being able to suggest viable solutions to his or her creative problems. For instance, how do you summarise the values of the client in a photo? This is where storytelling comes in handy. The other unsaid quality which clients highly appreciate is reliability. Always honour what you promise, wear the right clothes to the right occasions, and try to never be late for assignments. There are some clients who recognize my artistic pursuits but most just want a reliable – and sometimes creative – solution to their immediate problems.

We get a sense of the challenges of venturing out and the price one pays for taking the road less travelled. In your case, however, there have also been rewards. Your work, for a start, has been recognised internationally. To you, beyond personal satisfaction, what would you say is the larger significance of the global recognition?

Global recognition affirms my inner desire to "do well". So yes, there is personal satisfaction. Still, I think we should not be too obsessed with accolades and external validation. From my own experience, the international awards didn't get me very far. My clients didn't hire me because I won this award or that award. They hired me because they trusted me and enjoyed working with me. So the larger significance, ironically, is awards do more for your inner self than for your outer self. People quickly forget what you have won, but they seldom forget their experience working with you! (***Editor's Note:** Edwin's works have been exhibited at international photo festivals and exhibitions in countries like the Netherlands, France, China, Cambodia and Germany.*)

There are works that are personal and there are works that are commissioned, works that are long features and those that are more commercial. In your case, apart from the in-depth personal projects we have been talking about, you have also been published in international titles such as GEO, International Herald Tribune, The New York Times and Le Monde. Can give us a sense of how some of your global opportunities came about? From the practical perspective of career development, what would be your broad advice to young graduates who want to go beyond the local scene (and I am not referring to just those who plan to pursue photojournalism)?

These opportunities for me came about because I knocked on doors. Sometimes, it just takes that first person to believe in you for other doors to open. I recall pitching my first story to a Taiwanese magazine called

Rhythms (经典) and they paid me USD 2,000+ to publish my story on the Tibetans in Nepal. For GEO, I met the photo editor in a photojournalism workshop in Vietnam. I was nominated to represent Singapore by my photojournalism professor, Shyam Tekwani. That happened in 2004 when I just joined SPH. For IHT and NYT, I met the editors at a photo festival in France in 2009, when I went there to receive my Getty Images prize money. Le Monde came through my photo agency. My advice to young graduates is: be helpful and humble to everyone you meet. Win friends whenever you can. Do all this genuinely and not just because they may give you job opportunities later on. People can sense it if you befriend them for benefits. Don't do that! Just be genuine and sincere. In the end, these qualities will help you tide through life.

Next let's hear about Captured Pte Ltd, a Singapore-based photographers' collective which you and some friends started in 2013. I am not sure if you consider that as a move towards enterprise. How is your photographers' collective different from the businesses out there offering similar services? How do you try to balance practical considerations and what one may term artistic ideals?

When I started Captured, its mission was to help photographers like me stay afloat in our struggle for artistic excellence. The goal remains the same today. I have seen so often how people bail out or sell out. I don't want to do either – and I want to succeed with others. I believe there is strength in numbers. We are each other's sounding boards. We keep each other in check and inspire each other. Freelancing can be a very lonely endeavour and solitude itself can be a cause for ruin. No man is an island. So by banding together, we become more reliable service providers while inspiring each other to persevere in our personal work.

One area you have been involved in but which has not been covered much is mentoring. For example, in 2012, you, as Principal Mentor, founded the Kathmandu Inside Out (KIO) masterclass – an annual photography workshop

in Nepal. Why did you venture into mentoring? What was the impetus for your project in Kathmandu and what has been most satisfying about it?

I started KIO for two reasons: to give myself a legitimate excuse to go back to Nepal every year and to share my passion for storytelling with others. Mentoring is a very big word to use – I would say "coaching". Many people want to use photography to tell stories but few have the same fortune that I have had in terms of experiences. Many people take great photographs but photography remains a hobby because it doesn't "bring in the dough". Others just want to "try for fun" but don't know where or how to start.

With KIO, I repurpose the same methodology which I adopt for my own personal work and "make it work" by involving a community of Nepalese friends for the eight-day workshop. So in a way, I am magnifying my passion for storytelling through teaching. I am still amazed by the photo essays that my students come up with every year. And many of them came out of KIO with a higher level of appreciation for documentary photography. That is the most satisfying part of this project – changing lives, one photo at a time.

Editor's Note: *This project involves teaching visual storytelling through a hands-on, partnership-based methodology. By pairing participants with local photographers in Nepal, the workshop provides a platform for participants to challenge themselves to make meaningful pictures, beyond postcard perfection.*

Apart from the KIO initiative in Nepal, you have also undertaken other community projects locally. For instance, there was the *Island Nation* project in 2014 which you undertook with fellow photographers Juliana Tan and Zakaria Zainal to track former islanders from our Southern Islands who were moved to HDB flats on the mainland from the 1970s onwards. Then there was *Transit* in 2015, which aimed to, as you put it, "capture the daily theatre" of Singapore's multi-racial passengers on board its Mass Rapid Transit (MRT) trains. More recently, we had *One Portrait*, a community outreach project providing dignified photographic portraits to the elderly, especially those living below or close to the poverty line. Can you say more about the impetus for such projects?

In essence, *Island Nation* was an opportunity to find out things not mentioned in history books, to tell the stories of those aging islanders before it was too late. It was humbling to witness their affinity with the natural world – something hard for younger Singaporeans used to living in cities to imagine. There were some stirring moments, such as the one which happened during a trip to St John's Island we organised for a group of former residents. As I recounted in an interview with Tatler: "One lady in her seventies was brought to the beach in her wheelchair. The moment she saw the water, she stood up, went into the sea fully dressed, and started swimming very gracefully. She was so happy to be home. It was unforgettable."

As for *Transit*, it came after I returned to Singapore following my stint in Nepal. After being away, I had felt that my homeland was a very different country. The feelings of change were intense but how did they find expression? Not surprisingly, the inspiration would come from my past. The MRT, you see, has special meaning for me perhaps because I grew up beside a train station. I would watch the old trains pass by my window everyday. So quite naturally, I guess, I was drawn to them for my photography. I found that the trains had become so crowded that it was difficult to board them during peak hours. Out of frustration, I started to photograph what I saw at the doors.

The idea was simple. As I explained in a BBC interview: "If you commute on the MRT and we are forced two inches in front of the doors, we'd all have the same reactions and share the same expressions and vulnerability." In a way, *Transit* captured that shared but easily overlooked experience. This was how I explained the project on its website when it was launched: "As commuters (generally), we distract ourselves endlessly with our smartphones or iPads, to anaesthetise ourselves from the unnatural and uncomfortable experience of transit. We create private spaces for ourselves in the most public of spaces. As commuters, we observe an unspoken rule not to stare at each other's misery. As a photographer, I broke that last rule twice over – I recorded the stare, and continue to be amazed by what the stare reveals."

As for *One Portrait*, an initiative by our team at Captured in 2021, the goal was to give seniors in Singapore a framed portrait and, in the process, affirm their basic human dignity. I had explained to The Straits Times in an interview: "We call it (the project) *One Portrait* because we want to create that one portrait that represents the one gift that photography can give to our recipients. Some of the seniors have quipped that the photo taken of them is the one portrait that would end up at the head of the hearse on their final day."

Finally, Edwin, as a documentary photographer, you are best known for your black-and-white pictures or what has been termed your "evocative monochrome imagery" – with works that reveal "deeply rooted social issues and raw human emotions, blurring the lines between fact and fiction". Why black and white? Why social issues? Why the blurring of lines between fact and fiction?

I once came across this quote: "Sometimes, there is more truth in fiction than fact". I find this saying to be true. Some news reports are proven false when new developments surface. And while novels are fiction, they are usually a collection of real life truths put together in a creative way. In a way, this is what photographs do for people – everyone reads a photograph differently. Even though the subject of the photograph remains the same, the same photo shown to different people takes on different meanings. Still, there is a universality in the divergence – the emotions conveyed. Photographs are great at conveying emotions. Photographs are very truthful in this aspect because they transport you across time and space to experience viscerally a nugget of history. But this experience is filtered differently in different people. So is a photograph fact? Yes. Is experiencing a photograph fiction? Yes! Because we "imagine" what it was like and are informed by our own biases. That is why it is important to make long term personal projects – time distills the truth, and the truth is not one moment but a continuum. A substantial number of well-taken photographs, curated properly in a thoughtful manner, is capable of giving us a rather truthful account of history, no matter how subjective the photography is.

CHANGING LIVES

Picture courtesy of Edwin Koo

"I started the KIO (Kathmandu Inside Out) masterclass - an annual photography workshop in Nepal - for two reasons: to give myself a legitimate excuse to go back to Nepal every year and to share my passion for storytelling with others. Mentoring is a very big word to use – I would say 'coaching'. Many people want to use photography to tell stories but few have the same fortune that I have had in terms of experiences. Many people take great photographs but photography remains a hobby because it doesn't 'bring in the dough'. Others just want to 'try for fun' but don't know where or how to start. With KIO, I repurpose the same methodology which I adopt for my own personal work and 'make it work' by involving a community of Nepalese friends for the 8-day workshop. So in a way, I am magnifying my passion for storytelling through teaching. I am still amazed by the photo essays that my students come up with every year. And many of them came out of KIO with a higher level of appreciation for documentary photography. That is the most satisfying part of this project – changing lives, one photo at a time."

—Edwin Koo

CALL TO ARMS

"My father's well-loved copy of Eric Newby's classic came to me in the late 1990s. My parents, both accomplished travellers and authors, had spent the past 28 years trying to convince me that I could and should do anything but follow in their footsteps, wanting to spare me the rejection letters and overdrawn bank balances. The gift of Newby's book signalled a change of heart in my father, who then became a fierce advocate for my writing. It came at just the right moment. Like Newby, I was in a soulless job, desperate for change and adventure. Reading A Short Walk *was a revelation. The superbly crafted, eccentric and evocative story of his Afghan travels was like a call to arms. I quit my job, secured a book contract with Penguin, and headed to the Arctic. Newby's book continues to be my endlessly inspiring companion."*

KARI HERBERT ON *A SHORT WALK IN THE HINDU KUSH* BY ERIC NEWBY

Source: The Guardian

GLOBAL WORKPLACE

Picture courtesy of Shannon Teoh

"Working for a global newswire agency (marked a new learning curve for me). This experience exposed me to the global workplace. Until then, I only had Malaysian bosses. Now I was facing HQ in Hong Kong and was mostly supervised by Europeans and Americans. I learnt a lot as you don't do the same things in news gathering when in Malaysia compared to other places like the US, UK, France or China. The reporting cultures, the pressures of the job – they were also very different. We had to meet the KPIs from a distance, writing for a very general audience – some who might not even know Malaysia's exact location, much less the current affairs of the region. I learnt how stories about crocodiles biting a worker relieving himself by the river would light up the metrics far more than an update on the national GDP. I also learnt how the developed world's lens on other markets can be very set and entrenched. A lot of stories about Malaysia contextualised things in a cliche I would use over and over again - Muslim majority Malaysia – as if that could explain all the intricacies of what was going on. It was deeply challenging to get salient points across, given the very tight copy - often about 400 words - we had to work with."

—*Shannon Teoh*

CHAPTER 8

Drive & Curiosity

Shannon Teoh
Malaysia Bureau Chief

Pictures courtesy of Shannon Teoh

Shannon, let's start on an instructive note. At the annual Singapore Press Holdings (SPH) English/Malay/Tamil Media (EMTM) Group Awards in March 2021, you were awarded Story of the Year for your piece, "Malaysians await outcome of meeting over state of emergency". The story was published in October 2020, amidst Malaysia's political turmoil after then Prime Minister Muhyiddin Yassin met the king to explore imposing emergency measures. As those in the news business know, it takes a lot – of time, efforts, resources and attributes such as drive and curiosity – to land a good story. Can you give us a glimpse of the process that went into an award-winning piece, focusing on what you had to draw out from yourself in particular to produce such a story?

Firstly, no good exclusive just lands on your lap. You would have had to build relationships with contacts or position yourself in such a manner that a whistleblower might trust you with the valued information you want. So the genesis of such stories would have started in the past. You can think of a journalist's resources in the same way you might any balance sheet – whether you expend them on operating costs to produce something for today's news or invest them as assets for potential harvest in the future.

In this particular instance, I was tipped off by one contact the night before but certainly it was much too dangerous to go on a single source. A national emergency is a serious and rare occurrence, with the last one only called after the tragic race riots on May 13, 1969. So I metaphorically knocked on every door I could think of to try and confirm the tip off I was given. There were two possibilities. It would come to nothing and I would've wasted my time. Or it would be true and I would have a huge scoop. Again, these are gambles that journalists have to take. In the long run, hopefully the law of averages allows for some of these leads to bear fruit and make up for the ones that are rotten.

Editor's Note: *Shannon would go on to outdo himself. In February 2022, he was named Journalist of the Year at SPH Media Trust's (SMT) annual journalism awards for its English/Malay/Tamil Media Group. This time, what earned him the nod was his exclusive story on how Malaysian Prime Minister Ismail Sabri*

Yaakob had offered his rivals reforms in return for their support in Parliament. It all started when he heard about how the PM would be meeting top opposition leaders last August. Given his experience and his deep understanding of the political landscape of Malaysia, he could sense that something big was brewing.

He delivered his breaking news even while the political leaders' meeting was ongoing and two weeks before the authorities confirmed this. On his win, he told The New Paper: "This is down to the support and team spirit of my colleagues at the Malaysia bureau. At the bureau, everyone has each other's backs. We cover for each other so that we can deliver exclusives and master a wide range of beats, from crime and security to politics and economics."

Apart from your award-winning stories, you have written many other news stories and features. Many include intriguing details which can surface only with a curious mind that is constantly probing and asking good questions. Using your own stories as examples and focusing on the importance of communication skills in the workplace, can you give us a sense of the approach you take when doing your job – from looking out for good stories to getting people to talk to drawing out details which may otherwise be buried?

Editor's Note: *For a sense of Shannon's writing, consider his story on how Malaysia, confronted with a healthcare system stretched thin by the Covid-19 pandemic, had to resort to desperate measures. Sungai Buloh Hospital, for instance, had to use a shipping container as a makeshift morgue due to the surge in deaths.*

Curiosity can drive a story but it needs a bit of creative thinking and ingenuity sometimes to actually water that seed and make it grow into a story. In the case of the story about Malaysia's desperate measures as it faced a growing healthcare crisis due to the Covid-19 pandemic, what was needed would be some extreme examples to bring the situation to life. Everyone knew ICUs were overflowing and exceeding capacity but how would we draw a picture that people could understand? Enter containers as morgues, the military stepping in with field ICUs, and parking lots being used to quarantine patients with light symptoms. Anyone can see that these were unusual measures. The key thing here was stitching them together to show how dire the situation had become.

To an extent, any good story is still the result of an inquisitive mind – asking yourself the intriguing questions first so that you know what you are looking out for when you do your research and reporting. Certainly, asking newsmakers the right questions is also important. Any reporter is guided by the five Ws and one H, but these are just stepping stones towards the big one – "So what?". Why should anyone care about this story? Sometimes newsmakers just want to get their point and narrative across, and don't realise that nobody else cares. It is to their benefit, in fact, if they listen to the reporter, who is trying to get them to tell people why a particular story is a big deal.

When Malaysia launched its Covid-19 vaccination programme, for example, a third of those surveyed by the Health Ministry were reluctant to take the jabs. In the press conference, I had posed a question which was supposed to be answered by the minister in charge of the programme but the then Prime Minister, Muhyiddin Yassin, stepped in to take it. He took pains to explain that it was not just about saving lives but saving the economy. People, he said, would eventually take the dose as they may find themselves ostracised. I thought this was a great point that hadn't been made by the government before. They had simply been trying to convince people the vaccines were safe. But more than that, people were motivated by their own self-interest. So telling them that not taking the jabs would disadvantage them was probably the single best campaign message.

Next, let's get a sense of your career. An SPH write up describes you this way: "Shannon Teoh cut his teeth in print, web and wire agency journalism before joining The Straits Times in 2014, after a decade of covering everything from pop culture to politics, money to motoring". The range of skills from years in the trade would include research, network-building, management and video/photography for both online and print media. All this reflects diversity – whether with regard to the different media platforms, subjects covered or other broader skills, including people management. **What accounts for your high comfort level with regard to diversity? Can you give us a glimpse of influences from your younger days?**

I would say I have always been a curious person – the kind who can't sleep at night if there's some mental itch that needs scratching. In this sense, Google has helped me get countless hours of sleep because I can be kept up at night if I can't recall the word for something, let alone an actual piece of trivia. Also I've always been "up for it". I like trying different things in different aspects of my life. In sports, my main passion, for example, may be football. But growing up, I dabbled, sometimes competitively, in a wide range of sports – including track and field, chess, badminton, table tennis, basketball, handball and cycling. In terms of education and career, I too have been somewhat adventurous. I got a degree in electronics engineering but, while studying, I was freelancing for newspapers and magazines.

My first fulltime job was for the New Straits Times. As a large national newspaper, it had many different sections and I tried my hand at writing about all sorts of things. No subject was off limits and I found myself covering entertainment, crime, politics, food, technology, motoring, and even fashion and beauty. People often ask me why I decided to be a journalist. After all, if I had been an engineer or if I had gone into finance, where engineers are valued for their analytical skills, I would be much better off financially. My reply is this: Journalism is like a paid scholarship. In most cases, you pay to learn and then you're graded on the report you write. As a reporter, I get to learn things before others do and then I'm paid for the report I write.

Editor's Note: If Shannon is professionally versatile, that may have something to do with his hobbies. Take, for instance, his taste in terms of cultural offerings. This is how he describes them: "I am a big fan of Radiohead, Mogwai, Haruki Murakami and Tolkien, and have geeked out for decades over the Matrix, Star Wars and Terry Practchett's creations, especially the Discworld".

Let's go chronological next and get a sense of your career. With an engineering degree from Multimedia University in Malaysia, you went into journalism, joining the New Straits Times in February 2004 before leaving in July 2008. I understand a lot was packed into those four over years. **Looking back, what would you say were the best learning points from your stint at the New Straits Times? Did your lack of background in terms of training make things difficult or was that instead helpful in some ways? Did the fact that you already had a rich history of freelance work even before graduating help? More fundamentally, what personal traits have enabled you to multitask (with ease or otherwise)?**

Editor's Note: At the New Straits Times, among other things, Shannon was tasked with coordinating and managing content for its weekly music and motoring sections. This role included copy editing and working out cohesive and attractive packages; coordination of reporters, photographers, sub-editors and graphic designers; incorporating creative angles and attractive presentation styles; and news coverage and even photography. As News Feature Writer, he "analysed current events and covered the landmark 12th Malaysian General Elections that saw unprecedented losses for the ruling regime".

My background helped a lot. As I have mentioned, I would say I have traits like drive and curiosity which will certainly help any reporter. But I often tell those who want to join this field that they need something else – they must be resourceful. I don't know if this is something innate or can be taught but basically it's a bit like an engineer's job. You're presented with a problem and you have to troubleshoot and problem solve – as straight forward as that. It doesn't matter whether you have to develop a widescreen TV that is thinner than your competitors' or you have to find a way to tell a story when the information isn't right in front of you.

There's usually more than one way to skin a cat and that's incredibly important in places like Malaysia, where there is an Official Secrets Act rather than a Freedom of Information regime. If the general landscape is one where people don't want to be transparent, you will have to find ways around that. So whether it was dealing with content management for a section or multitasking between writing and corresponding with newsmakers as well as colleagues, I think my background did help with problem solving and management of priorities and time.

At the New Straits Times, one of the things I learnt was that if you want to achieve something, you can't really rely on your supervisors to hold your hand. I had some good editors and they helped facilitate the things I wanted to do. But I had to want to do them to begin with. I pushed myself hard. I recall there were times I was producing three to four times the content colleagues on the same desk were. It's not necessarily about being naturally hardworking. I would actually describe myself as lazy. But if there's something I am passionate about, then I'll want to pursue it doggedly.

All this did prepare me for future middle management positions. Knowing that you can't really control things like salary and perks, what you can do to motivate those under your care is to help make the link between them and upper management as smooth and pain free as possible. Often this may mean you absorb the pain. It may also mean knowing what makes those under you tick and helping them build their strengths even as they work on overcoming their weaknesses.

The fast pace of journalism often means lack of time and space for reflection. In 2009, you took time off from Malaysia news to pursue postgraduate studies after being awarded the Chevening Scholarship given by the British Foreign & Commonwealth Office. You focused on political communication at the School of Oriental and African Studies in London. What, for you, would be the main takeaways from the time exploring the academic circle – which is vastly different from the media world – in a foreign land? Citing some examples, in what ways was your curiosity for learning – perhaps of a different sort – piqued?

To be honest, the main motivation for the break was to have a sabbatical and take stock of not just my career but also my life. I don't actually think the Masters helped boost my career prospects since I went back to the same job after graduating. But it did help me grow as a person, I think, and to understand better the work I was doing and its place in the wider scheme of things. Being in the UK, especially London, opened my eyes first-hand to different cultures in a cosmopolitan city. The course I did challenged my thinking about the way things worked. I consumed a wide plethora of art, both produced and performed, travelled to new places and participated in societies and groups that I would not have back in Malaysia. One of my best memories was sitting front row in the cheap day seats for *Waiting for Godot* and coming up close with a living legend, Sir Ian McKellen.

I began reading up on critical theory and philosophy to understand what media does and how it works to shape individual realities. I also learnt about new sources of information as I gained exposure to academic journals, intellectual texts and communities of people with their own specialized knowledge. Social media today is new, vast and scary. But I think what I learnt during my Masters did help me digest the rapid changes we are all experiencing in a more considered manner. True to my curious nature and my tendency to try new things, I also took an elective on the economic development of Southeast Asia without having any background in economics. It was the toughest unit for me and brought down my grade average but I learnt a lot that has helped me in my work even now.

Next came your stint as Assistant News Editor/Senior Correspondent at The Malaysian Insider between 2008 and 2012. The roles were diverse but let me focus on two things. One, can you give us a glimpse of the adrenaline rush and the intensity involved when breaking big stories? Two, how did you venture into column writing and how has it helped you to develop your "personal voice"?

Editor's Note: At The Malaysian Insider, Shannon served as deputy to the Executive Editor for tasks such as clearing copies, working out story ideas, assigning reporters, content planning and manpower management. He covered news related to politics and the economy and wrote lifestyle features as well as columns from time to time. Other responsibilities included photography and "travelling across Malaysia and beyond at times, parachuting in to work under pressure on breaking stories that make national headlines".

Yes, the main role at The Malaysian Insider involved both deputising for the editor and at times running the entire newsroom on my own. At the same time, I still had to ensure I had lots of output myself. Looking back, I take some pride in how I coped with the demands of my various – sometimes conflicting – roles then. I was conscious about not letting my productivity drop in terms of stories, including exclusives, generated. That meant pushing myself hard but it was a great feeling to break a story and see other reporters try to follow up and match it. Given the online news cycle, sometimes you could see this (the rush of competition) happening right in front of your eyes – an exclusive got published while reporters at the same location rushed to speak to the newsmaker you just had tea with.

When you go for exclusives, you of course also have to be very careful with making new claims. There's a lot of concentration involved in making sure you don't slip up – not just in making sure that the facts are right but also that you've done all your checks and requests for comment. This kind of rush is something editors leverage on. Frankly there is often little reward. Instead, you're then asked how come you have missed some other stories. In my current position as a bureau chief, I often tell my editors: You can't expect our small team to match the hundreds or thousands of reporters out there. But we can try to ensure you get the best bang for your buck. Win some, lose some but win more than you lose.

As for how I started column writing, I think it was more to take the pressure off a bit. It was a nice contrast to the constant news flow where you must report everything as objectively as possible. Generally, the idea for me is this – sometimes things are just too infuriating or there is a point everyone is missing. So you need to get your view or views across. Not being a fulltime opinion writer, I don't think so much about personal voice. A lot of people are working in echo chambers, saying things their readers are already thinking. That's not wrong but I believe opinion pieces are great avenues to challenge preconceived notions. But we live in a world now where people just want to affirm their own perspectives.

Following your time at The Malaysian Insider, you joined Agence France-Presse as a correspondent based in Kuala Lumpur between July 2012 and July 2014. This involved covering Malaysia for a global newswire with content reaching over 150 different markets. Among other things, you travelled across the country to cover general, human interest, economic and political news and features. Broadly, how was working for a global newswire agency different from what you had been exposed to before? From the perspective of communication skills in particular, including working with people from different cultures, what new learning did this new role offer you?

This experience exposed me to the global workplace. Until then, I only had Malaysian bosses. Now I was facing HQ in Hong Kong and was mostly supervised by Europeans and Americans. I learnt a lot as you don't do the same things in news gathering when in Malaysia compared to other places like the US, UK, France or China. The reporting cultures, the pressures of the job – they were also very different. We had to meet the KPIs from a distance, writing for a very general audience – some who might not even know Malaysia's exact location, much less the current affairs of the region.

I learnt how stories about crocodiles biting a worker relieving himself by the river would light up the metrics far more than an update on the national GDP. I also learnt how the developed world's lens on other markets can be very set and entrenched. A lot of stories about Malaysia contextualised things in a cliche I would use over and over again – Muslim majority Malaysia – as if that could explain all the intricacies of what was going on. It was deeply challenging to get salient points across, given the very tight copy – often about 400 words – we had to work with.

In August 2014, you joined The Straits Times and are now its Malaysia Bureau Chief. This involves you travelling across the country to cover general, human interest, economic, political and security news and features, using text, photos and videos. Apart from the traditional traits needed in good, old journalism, this role increasingly also requires you to be well-versed in social media – eg you need to be adept at using content-management systems for web publishing. You seem to have struck that balance between the old and the

new well. **For you, what has been most satisfying as you navigate the new demands of the media world while maintaining its traditional strengths? More broadly, what general advice would you offer the young as they enter an increasingly complex working landscape?**

I think at the end of the day, what is required of a reporter, or any worker, is an end product that meets or exceeds the specifications demanded. No matter how digitalised the process gets, this will always be relevant. A business professional may have to analyse and parse through a lot more information now than before, and probably have less excuse to get things wrong. But that's part and parcel of everyone's life now. We want all the trappings of hyper-modernity, everything at our fingertips at a moment's notice. Well, guess what, somebody has to make that happen. So everyone has to do better, to live better. Otherwise, we might as well look for some communes or ashrams – if they are still around – where we can live a slower, Netflix-Amazon Prime-Spotify-iPhone-free life.

For my field, what has changed in the nearly two decades I've been doing this is that the pressure to produce has grown tremendously for reporters. My predecessors could sit comfortably after given much time to write a few stories. Now I have editors telling me that my bureau shouldn't complain if someone has to file three or four pieces when a big break happens – and produce his or her own visuals without depending on a photographer or videographer.

Perhaps what's changed for me as I have matured in the industry is this: While I used to be more excited about a particular opportunity or exclusive, now I look at the big picture more. I want to always be able to tell my editor that The Straits Times is providing the best coverage of Malaysia among foreign media. Sometimes it can be even better than local competitors. As long as I can honestly claim that, then I can feel justified in telling my bosses that my team loses some but wins more.

Malaysia's tourism campaign describes it as "Malaysia, Truly Asia". As someone who knows the country and its cities well, having lived there

and explored the nooks and crannies as a correspondent, how would you instinctively introduce it (or its people and cultures) to the curious-minded?

It's funny, this campaign. It is absolutely accurate that Malaysia probably has a wider breadth of accessible Asian cultures than anywhere else in the world. But it's also absolutely appalling how our mainstream tourism stakeholders then proceed to blank this reality out of existence. All the offerings are carefully curated so as not to offend the official narrative of Malaysia being a proper Muslim country, with other cultures allowed to "coexist harmoniously" because we have Chinatown and Little India and "everybody celebrates festivals together". I'm not sure all of Asia can necessarily be "harmonious". I think there is a clash and that's the beauty – how society negotiates these clashes and either accepts or rejects the compromises. There is definitely demographic violence in Malaysia and this is what makes it such an exciting place. And I have not even begun talking about exploring the various cultures and peculiarities of each state – even districts within states – and appreciating their different laksas, coffees, dances and animist beliefs that are being wiped out by officialdom.

Finally Shannon, in terms of the different states in Malaysia, taking some examples, how – at the expense of over simplification - would you distinguish each from the other as a quick way to stir a deeper interest in them among Singaporeans, for instance?

I think Singaporeans are most familiar with Kuala Lumpur, Johor Baru and Penang, each of which can be easily reduced to simplistic depictions. KL – most alike Singapore except dirtier and less efficient where you're not sure when the train is going to break down. JB – dash in, grab cheap stuff and try not to get into trouble in the process. Penang – the holiday destination of choice where you can still get "Singaporean" food. All these places are fine and worth visiting for sure.

But so few Singaporeans make it to east Malaysia. I know there is little interest as even from a reporting standpoint, the two states there are often neglected. But they are completely different, with specific food influences, amazing natural sights and languages. Some of the best scuba diving – and by extension seafood – is to be had here. Even the east coast of the peninsula is not one monolithic Malay heartland. Kelantan is fiercely different from everywhere else, including neighbouring Terengganu. It has less beautiful sea sides and greenery. While being the so-called most Islamist state, its own ancestral beliefs are also the most intriguing in Malaysia.

Perak is a beautiful balance of old and new. Melaka and Negri Sembilan play host to various minorities and practices that tell of a deep history whose continuity was broken by colonialism. Even north Johor is not the same as the "Iskandar"-ised south. As for Pahang, it may be less interesting as a demographic culture. But it offers a journey through the depths of the Peninsula, unveiling rivers full of freshwater fish, the best durian in the world and some excellent beaches as you come out onto the coast. Then as you travel south into eastern Johor, you start to encounter take off points to some of the most gorgeous island escapes you will find within driving distance of Singapore. Speak to people, visit their shops and homes, and you will find there is no real "Malay" or "Chinese" or "Indian" family, but rather subdivisions upon subdivisions. These are just colonial constructs being carried forward and in fact deepened by the establishment to ease its own work of keeping on top of things.

DRAWING A PICTURE

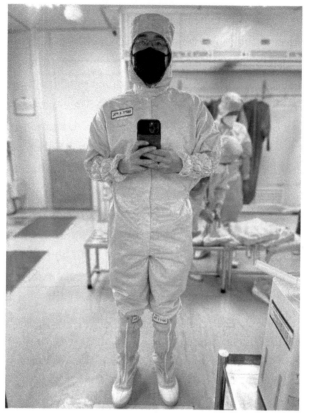

Picture courtesy of Shannon Teoh

"Curiosity can drive a story but it needs a bit of creative thinking and ingenuity sometimes to actually water that seed and make it grow into a story. In the case of the story about Malaysia's desperate measures as it faced a growing healthcare crisis due to the Covid-19 pandemic, what was needed would be some extreme examples to bring the situation to life. Everyone knew ICUs were overflowing and exceeding capacity but how would we draw a picture that people could understand? Enter containers as morgues, the military stepping in with field ICUs, and parking lots being used to quarantine patients with light symptoms. Anyone can see that these were unusual measures. The key thing here was stitching them together to show how dire the situation had become."

—Shannon Teoh

SENSE OF WONDER

"Reading this book for the first time, in London in 1989, inspired me to spend a summer rambling around the American west. The second time I read it 12 years later, I was stuck trying to write my first book. The subject was American nomadism. I had a box of notebooks about my encounters with modern-day nomads – freight train riders, cowboys, tramps, hippies, footloose retirees in motorhomes – and three shelves of research books about nomads in American history. How to connect all this into a whole? I saw that Frazier had solved a similar problem by using himself as a character – something I'd been resisting – and infusing his book with a sense of wonder. I sat down again with something to strive for."

RICHARD GRANT ON GREAT PLAINS BY IAN FRAZIER

Source: The Guardian

BOUNDLESS IMAGINATION

Picture courtesy of Clara Chow

"I'm very grateful for being able to go on residencies and spend time in the company of other writers and readers, and learn from them. Every chance to go somewhere new has taught me so much and changed me in fundamental ways. Each opportunity is so different. Toji was the first residency I did, and it completely changed my life, in the sense that I realised to be a writer is to live a life of discipline, determination and patience, which has nothing to do with external validation or financial reward. (In the case of) Rimbun Dahan, spending a month solo in a little garage-converted-to-house in Selangor jungle taught me that I was braver than I thought. Speaking to students, I have been given so much good energy and been impressed by their boundless imagination – I just want them to never have it drummed out of them. Making my way through the world, I try not to essentialise, so I really couldn't say what I've learnt about people collectively as nations compared to people I know in Singapore. Human beings are delightful; they also disappoint – it's the same everywhere. I would say that I really appreciate what has been invested in me in terms of these opportunities, and I want to keep working harder and put out work that is challenging."

—Clara Chow

CHAPTER 9

Draw of Cities

Clara Chow
Author/Editor

Pictures courtesy of Clara Chow

Clara, since this is a book about cities and curiosity, let's start with your two latest books – both of which can be broadly (if somewhat simplistically) described as travelogues. I am referring to *New Orleans* and *Caves*. Generally, can you give us a sense of your foray into travel writing (broadly defined) which is relatively new in Singapore? What makes you curious about the places you visit and what broader, deeper themes tend to surface for you?

I'm not sure I can say that such writing is new in Singapore. I was inspired by the work of poet Boey Kim Cheng, who once said in a workshop that travel writing, at its heart, is a quest – a search for an answer to a question specific to each of us (I hope I've paraphrased him accurately).

New Orleans started as a little joke between my friend, Argentinian playwright-director Santiago Loza, and I that we would write a little book "full of pictures". We just wanted to show our funding bodies, maybe, that we weren't slacking off while they sent us on these cultural exchange trips/writing residencies. But, of course, my motivation eventually wasn't that. Writing the book was a way of recording both what happened on the trip, our friendship, as well as my emotional and mental state in a particular point in time. So, you could say that my curiosity about the place I visited was ultimately curiosity about the people I was with and myself.

I remember walking down a street in the French Quarter, jazz blaring from the cafes, people spilling out onto the pavements, beads in the gutter – and I was just so happy, buoyed from all that energy, and just speaking to random people, asking questions. It stemmed from being swept up by an irrepressible joy – joy in being alive, no matter what the circumstances. That's the kind of city New Orleans is. It made me curious, rather than me already primed with questions when I arrived. Some places have the ability to change you. You just don't know how until you arrive. And then you go home and try and figure out why.

Similarly, *Caves* (which arguably could have just been titled *Ipoh*) happened because I just had this strange compulsion to go to Ipoh for much of my life. I went because I had to find out what it was inside me that made me want to go. And it turned out to be a journey inward, into the geological interior of cave temples but as well as into one's solitude as we were plunged into the pandemic and self-isolation.

Perhaps because places are made up of people (even, say, a deserted arctic outpost would bear a trace of human existence and community), I think I am ultimately curious about people and the human condition. Why do we want to keep living in the face of pain? Conversely, what does joy and sparkling perfection on the surface conceal?

Next, a bit more about *New Orleans*, a travelogue about a trip to the American city in October 2019. Published by Hermit Press, it has been described this way: "A Singaporean writer and an Argentinian playwright-director wander the streets of the French Quarter, being sober in a party town, singing on Bourbon Street, not gambling in casinos, dodging alligators in the bayou. It all ends with a gate-crash of Tennessee Williams' house. Along the way, some observations are made of art, friendship and being alive". Can you give us a sense of how the idea for the book, *New Orleans*, came about and the creative process behind it?

Actually I wrote that description as marketing copy – it was just a neat way of summarising it to sell the book, and I don't know if I did a good job of it. The impetus for the book I've mentioned above, and the creative process was – to me, at least – sit down at my squat table in my room every morning and scribble in my Moleskine notebook with a fountain pen, until I had put down everything that happened from beginning to end, hopefully in a way that did not bore the reader. That was pretty much it. The writing took a few weeks, and then I transcribed it, edited, proof-read and designed the book layout and cover. It really kept me sane during the circuit breaker in 2020.

In a Business Times piece, Helmi Yusof notes: "(*New Orleans*) took readers on a trip into the mythical American city. But it was also a trip into Chow's psyche, as she confronted her long-standing feelings of inadequacy as a writer, wife and mother. Readers identified with her struggles and e-mailed her letters of consolation and gratitude". How do you read the warm response

to *New Orleans* which was a modest hit among readers, briefly charting on Kinokuniya's bestsellers list?

I was extremely moved that Helmi found the book in a bookstore and read it. That was enough for me: that one person read it and understood. It kept me going. Writing is like dropping precious things down a very dark hole and listening for when it lands, if at all. You have to enjoy letting go. Everything else is a bonus. That said, I hope the book continues to be found by anyone who needs to read it. I hope it can give them a tiny bit of comfort.

Still on cities and curiosity, let's talk more about *Caves*, also published by Hermit Press. A travel memoir, it takes readers to various places in Ipoh, including its famous Taoist and Buddhist cave temples such as the Perak Cave Temple, Sam Poh Tong Temple and Nam Thean Thong. The obvious question is: How much is there to mine in a fairly familiar city near us? What does a curious mind see that most people don't? A message – if any – for the young looking for opportunities in an increasingly complex and uncertain world?

I can't in full conscience say that there was very much to mine in the touristic or journalistic sense. Ipoh, to me, just felt like a mood: the blue of the deserted traffic intersection, cast by a blazingly bright sari shop, at midnight; the vines snaking up peeling paint on empty shophouses; the lazily turning fan in a pink beer saloon. I think it was a lesson in anti-curiosity, maybe? That at some time you have to say that, okay there's really nothing much to sniff out as a self-respecting newshound here. Just relax and enjoy it and trust that you have something to write about, even if it's not spectacular? I don't even think I planned to write anything when I went there. It was on hindsight, when the borders were shut, and I thought: the last place I went to was IPOH? Okay, let's work with that and see what we can say about it.

The young looking for opportunities? I guess I'd say that if it sometimes feel like there are no opportunities out there and you've tried your best, it may sound counter-intuitive, but rest and conserve your energy. Mentally go to Ipoh, maybe. So that when it's time to be hungry again, you'll be recharged and ready.

To be fair, *Caves* isn't just a travelogue. Yes, at one level, it explores cave temples, bank vaults and a supposedly-haunted castle in Perak. But it also offers more. As Helmi Yusof notes: "(The book) is laced with ruminations on other writers' words and insights, such as Plato's allegory of the cave, the myth of Odysseus confronting the cave-dwelling cyclops Polyphemus, and Saramago's novel *The Cave*. It is also a journey into Chow's interiority, as she ponders – among many other things – her own relevance as an artist." **Can you tell us more about these bigger themes? How does one ensure that the depth explored – including heavy allusions – engages readers in our restless times?**

I didn't consciously think in terms of big themes while writing – the aim is to unpretentiously tell a story, and if there's something helpful to be gleaned, I trust the reader to do so for themselves.

The question of accessibility takes us to one of your other works, *Modern Myths*. Published in 2018 by Math Paper Press, it is a collection of stories that explores the pain and dilemma of modern living. **Using *Modern Myths* as an example, how do you handle the often contending demands of good writing – eg colour for engagement vs impeccable clarity of message?**

Editor's Note: In Modern Myths, figures from Greek mythology take up residence in contemporary Singapore as Clara explores big questions: "What happens when you are doomed to repeat your actions over and over? Or have to re-make your decisions, knowing that times have changed? What if struggling makes the divine human, and the human divine?" In an interview credited to an online source, she has explained her use of Greek myths this way: "I have always liked (them), for their ideas of transformation and also the very human emotions and behaviour of the less-than-perfect gods, so I just found that I kept taking them out of their traditional story containers and putting them in new situations. It started with Medea and then Orpheus, and soon I had a whole bunch of these stories, at which point I decided to put together the collection."

This question on accessibility is a difficult one for me to answer. I write in order to tell the story, and if my writing is tangled or gets in the way of the reader understanding what is happening, then I need to work harder to be clearer. But I also need to assume that there is a reader out there – even if it's just one – who will understand what I'm trying to say in the way I choose to say it.

Next, let's look at your debut collection of short stories in 2016. Titled *Dream Storeys*, it was inspired by imaginary buildings. What strikes me is that it is – as the publisher, Ethos Books, puts it – "a hybrid of journalism and fiction which documents the voices of urban visionaries while taking their ideas into inventive, evocative new territories". Can you give us a glimpse of the genesis of *Dream Storeys* and the process behind it?

Dream Storeys happened because I was making the transition from journalism to creative writing. It was a bit frightening to be on your own, without an editor to give you a brief. So I thought I'd be my own editor and give myself a brief: talk to some architects about their unbuilt plans for buildings in Singapore (this was in the run-up to the SG50 celebrations, so the idea was to also speculate about a kind of alternative physical and social landscape for the years ahead, after that milestone).

And after I interviewed the architects, I wrote a short story set within that unbuilt/unrealised building or environment. It was a concept that gave me creative constraints within which I could structure original narratives. So I went out and interviewed people like I already knew how, and went home and tried to write stories, which I was still figuring out how then. I repeated the process about a dozen times, and then there was something like a book.

Reviewing *Dream Storeys*, Yeow Kai Chai, writing as co-editor at Quarterly Literary Review Singapore, eloquently notes, "I don't remember reading a

crossgenre title like this, wonderfully traversing creative fiction, research and documentation without hitting a clunky, postmodernist note. Clara Chow's agile blend of journalistic rigour and narrative empathy pays off handsomely. Rooted in reality and taking off into the heady realm of imagination, her stories are propelled by an urge to find a heart in the architecture of our lives, as characters navigate these dream structures, trying to find a human connection." **Can you give us a better understanding of what Yeow terms the "agile blend of journalistic rigour and narrative empathy"? In your case, where does that come from? A combination of your formal training in literature and your journalistic background?**

The honest answer to this is "Maybe? I don't know?" Thank you, Kai Chai, for being extremely kind and supportive. (***Editor's Note:*** *Educated at the National University of Singapore with a Bachelor of Arts in English Language and Literature as well as a Masters of Arts in Literary Studies, Clara was a correspondent and copy editor with The Straits Times.*)

At this point, it seems apt to look at your writing career more broadly. Professionally, you have experience in journalism, writing for The Straits Times, My Paper and the South China Morning Post. You have also served as a copy editor, "thwacking through the tangled bush that was raw reporter copy", as you have put it. **For those not familiar, can you say more about this lesser known side of your writing career (as opposed to your more familiar role as a creative writer)? What would you consider your more memorable stories and experiences? Going back further, how did you end up in journalism? In your case, were there clear signs in your primary/secondary/JC days that you would end up in a career in the arts (in particular journalism and writing)? What other options were entertained and then abandoned for whatever reasons?**

In primary school, I wanted to be a writer, and later I thought I wanted to be an actress. In university, I wanted to be an academic and read books forever. Family circumstances meant that I needed to work to help pay the mortgage and other loans immediately upon graduating. I applied for magazine and newspaper jobs, because it seemed the most immediately relevant thing someone would hire me and my arts degree for. It should be noted that I used to be unable to meet deadlines – my history tutor was exasperated that I would hand up essays weeks late or not at all. So journalism was never one of my ambitions.

But journalism taught me how to write to deadline. It taught me not to take it personally when people edit your stories, to consider all edits and feedback as potentially helping to strengthen the piece. It taught me that research and legwork are everything – having nothing interesting to write about is *always* worse than not being able to write evocatively or with proper punctuation. That one should get to the point quickly, if you can help it – there is grace in economy. That done is better than perfect.

Your role as creative writer has opened some global doors for you. For instance, your stories have appeared in Asia Literary Review, Columbia Journal, Litro UK, Shanghai Literary Review and Prairie Schooner. You have been writer-in-residence at the University of Iowa (USA), Toji Cultural Centre (South Korea), Bogong Centre of Sound Culture (Australia), Rimbun Dahan (Malaysia) and ASEAN Literary Festival/ASEAN-Japan Residency (Jakarta) as well as a speaker/facilitator/mentor for the Ministry of Education's Creative Arts Programme. Can you say more about these opportunities? What have you learnt about your country's (and people's) strengths and limitations in the course of your global interactions?

I'm very grateful for being able to go on residencies and spend time in the company of other writers and readers, and learn from them. Every chance to go somewhere new has taught me so much and changed me in fundamental ways. Each opportunity is so different. Toji was the first residency I did, and it completely changed my life, in the sense that I realised to be a writer is to live a life of discipline, determination and patience, which has nothing to do with external validation or financial reward. (In the case of) Rimbun Dahan, spending a month solo in a little garage-converted-to-house in Selangor jungle taught me that I was braver than I thought. Speaking to students, I have been given so much good energy and been impressed by their boundless imagination – I just want them to never have it drummed out of them.

Making my way through the world, I try not to essentialise, so I really couldn't say what I've learnt about people collectively as nations compared to people I know in Singapore. Human beings are delightful; they also disappoint – it's the same everywhere. I would say that I really appreciate what has been invested in me in terms of these opportunities, and I want to keep working harder and put out work that is challenging.

Editor's Note: One catches a glimpse of Clara's belief in not "essentailsing" from her description of her experience in 2017 mingling with a bunch of writers from various parts of South-east Asia during a residency programme in Kampung Muara, a village/suburb in Jakarta. As she notes in a column for The Straits Times: "Like a misguided anthropologist, I peppered my new friends with questions. How does the gender-determined inflections in the Thai language shape the way Thai people view categories of male and female? Does it mean more or less fluidity? How has national war and trauma influenced the way Vietnamese writers write? What does being bilingual bring to your writing? As the days went by, however, and I trudged around with a battalion of portable fans, in my sun hat, trying not to be a clumsy auntie and fall into wet cement again, I realised that none of my fellow writers-in-residence fit into easy categories. Bangkok-based Mai Nardone, who is half-Thai and half-American, is working on a novel centred on the politics of surrogacy. Intan Andaru, a popular novelist in Indonesia, is also a medical doctor who has worked in remote villages. Meiling Kogure, the daughter of a Chinese-Malaysian man and a Japanese woman, writes poetry and pop songs. Hariz Faddylah, a poet from Brunei and the youngest of our bunch at 20, writes angry poetry a la Allen Ginsberg and Chairil Anwar. He told me that it was reading Alfian Sa'at's poetry that made him realise that he, too, could publish and be heard. Check your essentialising baggage at the front door."

You have described your upcoming works this way: "Works-in-progress involve typewriters, joss paper, disappearing ink, Chinese poetry, East-Asian TV dramas, tarot cards, Rolodexes, cowboys, samizdat, honey, baroque music, acts of female fandom, over-policing of museum visitors, bone-folders, motherhood, orchids, AI translation and self-care." The way I see it, there is a lot of playful yet intellectual curiosity at play here. To you, what does the list say about you? Again, any thoughts – if any – for our young?

Wow! I think I wrote that bio/description fairly recently – it's a strange feeling to have it quoted back so quickly. Thank you for saying that list is playful. It really is what I hope for, to work on things that are first and foremost fun for me. Otherwise I am a professional procrastinator and nothing gets finished. I think I am interested in things that are ephemeral, that are old and in danger of disappearing. Things that are downright weird, trivial or often dismissed as unworthy of study because it is too mainstream/popular. I love to take a Google deep-dive into whatever happens to catch my attention at the moment – Google News and Scholar are my friends – and I have a Twitter account specifically for talking to K-pop fans of a specific (not-famous-outside-of-Korea) group.

I was talking to my husband and I said the worst thing I can ever say to our children when they tell me they want to do something is this: "Why on earth would you want to do that?" Life is hard enough. Mustering up the courage and energy to be enthusiastic about something is hard. So when someone tells me, whether that someone is young or old, that he or she has thought about it and wants to do XXX or YYY, I am going to say: "Do it. Do it now."

What I'm getting at is, if you're curious about something, anything, find out more. Google it on your phone. Don't make excuses for yourself not to follow a bee in a bonnet down the rabbit hole (mixing metaphors is allowed!). I imagine my friend Santiago asking me, whenever I hemmed and hawed about following through on my own plans: "You have anything better to do?" That's a legitimate question. Listen to your own answers.

Places have a way of evoking strong thoughts and feelings in us. You, for instance, have shared about how your trip to Ipoh drew out strong thoughts in you regarding your role as an artist amidst the current pandemic. **What are some compelling thoughts and feelings you have for some of the cities you have been to? Given that you have once described yourself as "a small-island girl in search of continents", what would you tell our young when they get the chance to explore the world again – either to live in cities or just visit them?**

Editor's Note: In a Business Times story published in 2021 on how travel books by Singapore authors were a hit during the pandemic, Clara shares parallels between her life and the city of Ipoh – the subject of her book, Caves: "Ipoh used to be a thriving place with tin mines and rubber plantations that made people rich. But the collapse of tin prices in the 1950s put Ipoh into some kind of a holding pattern. The Ipoh today is very different from the Ipoh it was then. In a way, that's how I view my life under lockdown – that it's in a holding pattern... But, at the same time, Ipoh tells me that I will be fine. Ipoh moved past its halcyon days, adapted to its slower rhythms and it's doing just fine. I think I can do the same."

My plans change all the time: at one point, I really wanted to live in Chengdu. Sichuan province – and the once-connected Chongqing special municipality – has a very distinct flavour to me, compared to Beijing in the north. Maybe because most Singaporean-Chinese are descended from ancestors from southern China, I felt really at home there. You could sit in a teahouse all day, with unlimited hot water and steep the heck out of one packet of tea leaves, and doze or daydream. Or you could go to an archaeological site and stare at weird alien-like masks. Or go to the park or malls and squeeze with a gazillion people, or sing karaoke late at night at the intersection of two misty rivers. I can't say exactly what it was that spoke to me about Chengdu, but there's a sense of being able to disappear into the crowd or into history.

Right now, I'm learning Korean, so that I can divide my time at a later point between South Korea and Singapore. At least, I'm hoping there will be an option to, given that working remotely is so convenient now and that the wonderful thing about being Singaporean is that our passports are welcome almost everywhere, often with no visa requirements. I think there's no way to really know a city unless you try to live there. Not forever, but at least a few months.

Finally, Clara, what would you tell those who are struggling with living a creative life during this pandemic?

It's always hard and unknown, and you won't know how something will turn out until you actually do it. Trust your instincts. If a sabbatical and some time out is what you need, then follow your heart and do what's best for you – that will always cancel out the cons. Guard your mental well-being and your time jealously. Be suspicious of people who tell you what you ought to do "for your own good". Do what *you* want. Question everything.

Julia Cameron's *The Artist's Way* is a book that has helped me a lot. The way I see it, creativity can't be stored or used up. You start making something, and the creativity comes. You don't; it doesn't. The tap turns on and off, giving you the amount you need. There's no need to even pay a water bill for it. The only thing that stops us from touching the tap is fear itself. We think: what will people think about the art I haven't started making? And that's when it seems like we won't be creative enough. But when we think: What do I want to make? How do I take the next step? Then the process has begun and creativity as a question or equation doesn't factor anymore. It's just a series of actions, plans, solutions. It may take time, but trust in the process. You know you've got this.

DISTINCT FLAVOUR

Picture courtesy of Clara Chow

"*My plans change all the time: at one point, I really wanted to live in Chengdu. Sichuan province – and the once-connected Chongqing special municipality – has a very distinct flavour to me, compared to Beijing in the north. Maybe because most Singaporean-Chinese are descended from ancestors from southern China, I felt really at home there. You could sit in a teahouse all day, with unlimited hot water and steep the heck out of one packet of tea leaves, and doze or daydream. Or you could go to an archaeological site and stare at weird alien-like masks. Or go to the park or malls and squeeze with a gazillion people, or sing karaoke late at night at the intersection of two misty rivers. I can't say exactly what it was that spoke to me about Chengdu, but there's a sense of being able to disappear into the crowd or into history. Right now, I'm learning Korean, so that I can divide my time at a later point between South Korea and Singapore. At least, I'm hoping there will be an option to, given that working remotely is so convenient now and that the wonderful thing about being Singaporean is that our passports are welcome almost everywhere, often with no visa requirements. I think there's no way to really know a city unless you try to live there. Not forever, but at least a few months.*"

—**Clara Chow**

PURE GENUIS

"This account of a journey taken in the 1950s, rediscovered in the 1980s by Eland Press, encapsulates, for me, the essence of good travel writing. Never shying away from describing the frustrations and discomforts of travel, Sybille Bedford is nonetheless quick as a hummingbird to suck the sweetness from every experience. She confesses she chose Mexico because she wanted 'to be in a country with a long nasty history in the past, and as little present history as possible', but it's her stay with Don Otavio, a bankrupt squire living in a backwater, that becomes the highlight. Her hilarious, pithy dialogues are pure genius."

ISABELLA TREE ON *A VISIT TO DON OTAVIO* BY SYBILLE BEDFORD

Source: The Guardian

FINDING A COMMUNITY

Picture courtesy of Warran Kalasegaran

"When I moved to Japan, learning a martial art was on my bucket list. I like sports and I wanted to try a Japanese activity. There was a dojo *near my home that taught* kudo, *a combination of karate and judo. Neither the instructor nor most of the students spoke English. At my first class, a senior student gestured to me to change into gym clothes. But as I was already changed, I misinterpreted him and took my shirt off! I started learning by watching my instructor and following his moves. Eventually, the first Japanese words I learned were about decimating someone – kick (keri), front kick (mae keri), knee (hiza). But I got to know my teammates better over the two years. At my first fight, they were at my corner, helping me warm up and encouraging me throughout the fight. I felt proud for learning a new skill. But given how much of an adjustment moving to Japan was, I felt even happier for finding a community."*

—Warran Kalasegaran

CHAPTER 10

Hearing Stories, Making Friends

Warran Kalasegaran
Author/Diplomat

Pictures courtesy of Warran Kalasegaran

Warran, you have been working at the Ministry of Foreign Affairs of Singapore since 2016 and are currently based in Kuala Lumpur. Before that, you, through your education, had the opportunity to be exposed to other cities – Warwick in UK and Tokyo in Japan. Broadly, what does being based in another place – with its unique cultures and mores – mean to you?

It is the differences among us that make the world colourful and interesting. I enjoy learning about how different places and communities developed different architecture or foods or political systems over time, and soaking in different experiences. This could be walking through the Akamon (Red Gate) to enter Tokyo University, trying durians in Pahang, or visiting Shakespeare's home near Warwick University and learning about the words he coined. Most of all, I like meeting people who come from different backgrounds, hearing their stories, and making friends. Eventually, it is that sense of friendship that no longer makes a place feel different or "other", but makes you feel like you could belong too.

When I moved to Japan, learning a martial art was on my bucket list. I like sports and I wanted to try a Japanese activity. There was a *dojo* near my home that taught *kudo*, a combination of karate and judo. Neither the instructor nor most of the students spoke English. At my first class, a senior student gestured to me to change into gym clothes. But as I was already changed, I misinterpreted him and took my shirt off! I started learning by watching my instructor and following his moves. Eventually, the first Japanese words I learned were about decimating someone – kick (*keri*), front kick (*mae keri*), knee (*hiza*). But I got to know my teammates better over the two years. At my first fight, they were at my corner, helping me warm up and encouraging me throughout the fight. I felt proud for learning a new skill. But given how much of an adjustment moving to Japan was, I felt even happier for finding a community.

You were at the University of Warwick between 2011 and 2014, studying Politics with International Studies. Following that, you pursued postgraduate studies (Master of Public Policy) in Tokyo University between 2014 and 2016. Looking back, what would you consider your strongest memories from these stints?

What I remember most about studying overseas must be time spent doing everyday things with friends. This could be catching a coffee break while studying at the library, playing drinking games and going on a night out, or having a snowfight at Leamington Park. I really enjoyed talking with my friends, from the deep conversations to the funny banter to anything in between. I also got to see parts of the world where my friends lived. I visited their homes in the UK and they brought me to climb the tor rock formations in Devonshire or row in the Thames in London. As I was learning Spanish at university, I did a homestay in Valencia one summer. I still have fond memories of arguing with my homestay family about the cruelty of bullfighting while eating up the amazing tortillas made by *abuela* (grandma). But it was the people that made everything special. I got to know my friends and their families better, and we became family too. Whenever my family visited, I introduced them to my friends as well. I am always happy to host my friends whenever they visit me and show them around what I boldly claim as "my cities" – wherever I happen to be based at a particular point in time.

You also had some valuable internship experiences. For example, as an undergraduate, you had internships in New York, Jakarta, and Seoul. Later, there was also an internship with the UN Environment Programme Finance Initiative in Switzerland, Geneva. Can you say more about your internship experiences? How important were they to the subsequent development of your career?

I was lucky to be offered a scholarship by the Ministry of Foreign Affairs (MFA) to go to university. I would not have been able to afford studying overseas, or tried many of the experiences I mentioned, without the financial support of the scholarship. It made many of these experiences possible. MFA also opened up opportunities like the internships. For all this, I am grateful.

The internships gave me a glimpse of MFA work, deepened my interest in the career I would eventually pursue, and helped me to build relationships in MFA before I joined full-time. As an intern, my capacity to contribute was limited. But I could watch what Singaporean diplomats did, learn some tradecraft like how to take notes, and hear them talk about their jobs. This piqued my interest to do more. The internships also let me make friends with people in MFA, especially the officers who were my mentors. When I eventually started work, it was nice to have a community of friends and mentors to return to. Having internships in different parts of the world also made me more confident of adapting to new environments. It could be getting a ride on a motorbike to get to office on time in Jakarta traffic. Or commuting from France to Geneva to intern at the UN Enivronment Programme Finance Initiative (UNEPFI) because of how expensive it was to stay in Switzerland itself. Or simply being able to relate to people from different parts of the world.

One example was my internship at the Singapore Permanent Mission to the UN in New York in 2012. It was interesting watching long, heated negotiations take place behind the scenes. For example, a UN translator had to ask one diplomat talking angrily to slow down so that she could keep up with the translation. Overnight negotiations would pause to celebrate a diplomat's birthday. The other diplomats always spoke well of the Singaporean diplomat who was my mentor. Experiences like this made me excited about doing more with MFA.

My internship at the UN Environment Programme Finance Initiative in Switzerland, Geneva, in 2016 was part of credit for my course in Tokyo University. I was amazed by the practical means UNEPFI came up with to get financial institutions to include sustainability as an investment principle. I got to sit in on phone calls with banks, or learn about how to quantify the financial cost of environmental risks in investments. But the highlight was meeting all the other UN staff and interns from all over the world. It was a very interesting and fun community, and I enjoyed getting to know everyone.

At the Ministry of Foreign Affairs, you are now First Secretary (Political) at the Singapore High Commission in Kuala Lumpur. Before this posting, you had some highlights. For example, you were involved in work at the World Trade Organisation and World Intellectual Property Organisation in Geneva,

and the World Economic Forum in Davos. You were also country officer focusing on Malaysia and Brunei. **Looking back at your earlier days, what was particularly challenging, given the level you had to operate at? How did you manage the steep learning curve? Generally, what traits would you say are particularly useful for young professionals thrown into the deep end – and in international waters too?**

I had several challenges when I first joined MFA. One was getting up to speed on the background for the various issues I covered. Foreign policy issues tend to have years of historical context that you need to catch up on fast. I couldn't make an analysis or a recommendation if I didn't know what happened in the past and why past decisions were made. Another challenge was staying on top of the high volume of work without missing any tasks or deadlines. I also had to learn to write the MFA way – short and to the point.

I made a lot of mistakes. I was lucky to mostly have had good bosses and teams, who advised me and did not make me feel little even when I got something wrong. I tried to pick up learning points from whatever happened, seek advice, read up on my own, and try harder the next time. Of course, you sometimes feel down or tired. My colleagues and I cheered each other on, and swapped stories about our mistakes. I dropped by at my grandma's place to eat or chilled out with my family and friends to recharge. Looking back, it was just about taking things in my stride. I learnt to keep going, come what may.

I am still learning though. I read new things about Malaysia and the world every day, or meet people who introduce me to different perspectives. Whereas previously I was focused on getting better at work, now I have also been trying to pay forward the support that I have received. This means looking out for other members of my team, for instance. I am trying to balance throwing myself into work with stepping away to look after my body and mind. I do this by doing yoga or making the effort to spend time with family and friends and being there for them too.

The traits I recommend are curiosity, confidence and kindness. Develop your interest in things both in and outside work. Read widely, try new things, and keep learning. Eventually they will converge to make you better in and out of work. You will make mistakes along the way, or your priorities may change. Be confident in your judgment to choose for yourself, trust your ability to learn and improve, and keep going. Be kind to yourself and look out for others at the same time. Work today is fast-paced and 24/7, and we are inundated with text messages, emails, and news updates. It is important to take time off and to look out for colleagues who are likely facing the same challenges. Build strong relationships at home, with friends, and at the workplace. These relationships will anchor you and ultimately be what matter. Pay it forward too. Trying to make a positive difference, small or big, to other people's lives – this is good in and of itself. But it can also bring perspective to the daily urgent demands of work.

Growing up, was the idea of an education and career beyond our shores always there for you? Who or what were some of your influences? More specifically, what global forces (for want of a better term) were you shaped by, consciously or otherwise, back when you were a secondary or JC student?

No, the idea of an overseas education or career was not always there for me. In fact, my alma mater Victoria Junior College (VJC) didn't accept me into its programme for potential scholars, although it may have made the right call then. A family friend who used to work at MFA came to see my grandmother when I was in VJC. He told me about his posting to Egypt. That left an impression on me – the travelling, meeting new people, seeing interesting things. That made me want to understand how the world worked and participate in it. When I completed JC, I applied for the MFA scholarship because I was genuinely interested in a job related to foreign affairs. Even then, the prospect of studying overseas and the other opportunities that it would open up still had not yet hit me. I am very thankful that I got the scholarship or I wouldn't know what I might have missed.

My influences growing up were very local and relational. My mum was the pillar of my household. From her I learned values like hard work, frugality and love. She made sure I studied hard and tried different things like art. She gave me a love for reading and writing, and taught me to be careful with language. My dad travelled a lot. When I was older, he talked to me about the news around the world. I found the world through his eyes interesting, and wanted to understand it better. My uncle was my role model. I aspired to dress and talk like him and do the adventurous things he did. Together, they motivated me to push myself and be confident. They took me on trips that made me think about the world outside. They are also kind and good people, and inspire me to be good to others and to give back where I can.

School was a localised experience too. It was defined by places like the street soccer courts, going to the computer gaming centre to play DOTA, or hanging out at Parkway Parade over a very good Oreo bubble tea. I joined a dance group and we enjoyed rehearsing in empty classrooms. But on hindsight, I picked up social skills, a joy for interacting with people, and strong friendships that anchor me till today. Even on the one school trip we took to England and France during JC that was supposed to be a literature programme, my strongest memory is more social than intellectual. I recall a bunch of us students sneaking out at night to see the Eiffel Tower, only to get lost and scared and doubling back. When I moved to Malaysia, one of the first things I did was reconnect with my Warwick University friends here and join their football team.

I think Singaporeans are well-suited to interacting with the world. We are raised with an understanding that Singapore is a small country that needs to engage the world smartly to survive. This has led to us thinking about the world from young. Singapore is also a place where differences reside together. My family is part Indian, Ceylonese, Chinese and Malay. We celebrate Deepavalli and Hari Raya. We speak English at home and crack Tamil jokes. My friends were from different backgrounds, with some from other countries as well. Growing up was all about learning about different people and places, and understanding that people – however different on the surface – are the same in the end.

Next, let's take a look at another side of you. I am referring to you as an author. While studying in Tokyo, you wrote your debut novel, *Lieutenant Kurosawa's Errand Boy*, which was longlisted for the 2016 Epigram Books Fiction Prize and shortlisted for the 2018 Singapore Book Awards (Best Fiction Title). Reports have suggested that your interest in the Japanese Occupation was sparked by having maternal grandparents who were orphans during that period and by your studies in Tokyo. **Can you give us a glimpse of how this book came about?**

Editor's Note: *Lieutenant Kurosawa's Errand Boy follows an eight-year-old Tamil boy forced to work for the Imperial Japanese Army during its occupation of Singapore. Reviewing the book in The Straits Times in 2017, journalist Olivia Ho writes: "While the story of the Japanese Occupation during World War II is the well-worn material of every Singaporean child's social studies textbook, one is hard put to find new ways of telling this age-old litany of horrors. Civil servant and first-time author Warran Kalasegaran manages to do so in this coming-of-age narrative of a young Tamil boy who is forced to work for the Kempeitai, the Japanese secret police, and, in doing so, must renounce his name and the culture of his birth....In Kurosawa's employ, Nanban suffers beatings and whippings as his new master indoctrinates him into the conqueror's culture, teaching him to speak Japanese, learn their martial arts and, over time, to exercise the Kempeitai's brand of brutality against others, including his own people. He forms a strange relationship with Kurosawa, to whom he is a mixture of son and slave....(What the novel does) is ask the vital question of what it takes to belong to a culture when one looks like one should not, what one learns, what one inherits and what one chooses to keep."*

There were several influences. Both of my mum's parents were orphans during the Japanese Occupation. I wondered what that period must have been like and how it shaped their view of the world. I was also studying in Japan and learning more about its history, and hearing classmates from all over the world discuss World War 2 in seminars. I wondered what my grandparents would make of what some of the students said about the Occupation, given their own personal experiences with it, and how different people have different views of this period in history.

My grandma, who is ethnically Chinese, was adopted by a Punjabi-Tamil family, and it was a hook to explore issues related to identity in such a diverse society. I started trying to connect these themes together in my writing, and I guess the fundamental question was, "What makes us who we are?". The final version of the story struck me on a bus ride – to tell a story about a Singaporean boy forced to work for a Japanese officer, and how this affected the boy; and of a Chinese girl adopted by an Indian family who meets this boy much later when she's part of Singapore's nascent independence movement.

In talking about *Lieutenant Kurosawa's Errand Boy*, you have said in an interview with The Straits Times: "It lets us tell stories about people who may have been missed out by historians – the poor, the illiterate, the minorities – and reclaims a space for them on the map of history." At the same time, in an interview with Centre For Stories, you have said: "I try to tell stories of Singapore through the eyes of the small Tamil community in English, and put Tamil heroes and heroines at the front of these stories." Can you say more about how you see your role as a writer? What has shaped your understanding of this role?

Representation is very important in the arts. The stories we tell cumulatively form a narrative that shapes the opportunities and challenges available to all of us. If stories keep painting Asians in one stereotype, sooner or later we fall into the trap of believing it, and it becomes a self-fulfilling prophecy. A lot of English-based media commit this crime. Worse still, they erase other people from the discourse altogether. One example is the contribution of Indian soldiers to both World Wars in Europe, which is entirely missing from a lot of English-media film and writing. Instead, we get a reinforcement of the narrative of the white hero while people from other regions are marginalized.

One of my recent short stories, "The Coat", is about an Indian soldier fighting in World War 1 France. In writing it, part of my aim was to correct this historical fallacy and restore representation and, in fact, truth. *Lieutenant Kurosawa's Errand Boy* dealt with issues of identity too. But the most important aspect of it was just to show characters who were Singaporean, make them heroes, and demonstrate that they were completely relatable to the reader.

I also enjoy telling stories about life in Singapore, showing how we play football in void decks, hang clothes out on bamboo poles or are surrounded by the beautiful shophouses in Little India. I hope to continue writing about people like me and reclaiming that space on the map for us. In the end, I hope people wandering the libraries in Singapore will see themselves in my stories.

In the same Centre For Stories interview, you have shared about your literary influences this way: "I read the usual culprits growing up. I remember Enid Blyton, Harry Potter, Artemis Fowl, and children's versions of epics like the Mahabharata. I had a serious fling with medieval fantasy and other ancient history-based dramas, like the *Lord of the Rings, Wheel of Time*, and Christian Jacq's Egyptian stories. We've broken up since." To update (if there is a need to), what would be your recommended list for today's young and why?

I usually recommend reading anything that interests someone, as long as he or she reads with a critical eye. If I were to choose a shortlist, I would definitely include the Indian epic, *The Mahabharata*. Although it is a long read, it has a lot of lessons about the complexity of life, choices and consequences. I enjoy reading fiction rooted in place and history, and normally read books by authors in the country I'm in at any point in time. *American Spy* by Lauren Wilkinson is an interesting take on the Black American experience. *The Sympathiser* by Viet Than Nguyen explores issues related to Asian identity in the US and the Vietnam War. In Malaysia, I enjoy reading Shih-Li Kow's stories.

You have identified *For Whom The Bell Tolls* by Ernest Hemingway as "a turning point" for you, citing his sharp and simple writing to go with a good plot and intriguing characters. You have added: "(Hemingway) taught me that good writing can be interesting and clean, and also gave me the confidence to read 'difficult' books and trust my judgment of them." Given such influence (or other similar influences), what do you keep in mind when you write or,

even more broadly, when you communicate – for instance, as a working professional in today's corporate context?

At MFA, I write with the reader in mind. The people I write to in MFA probably have many things to read. So I consider what they may want to know, what the key messages I want to convey are, and how I can communicate as succinctly as possible while making an impact. I reread and rewrite often, and take in comments from my team and bosses. With fiction, I write the story that interests me. There may be a theme to it, but at the start of the writing process, it is usually plot or character-driven. I try and go with the flow. But in the end, I also reread and rewrite often. I usually ask my sister or friends to read my stories and take in their comments too. Moral of the story: always rewrite!

On a lighter note, your Twitter write up says this about you beyond describing you as a diplomat and an author: "Break out randomly into dance, laugh hard, and am grateful." Can you elaborate and in the process give readers a glimpse of your personality and temperament?

I like to have a good time with the people around me, I try not to take myself too seriously, and I'm grateful for the opportunities I've had and the people I'm surrounded by. That said, I wrote that epithet before Covid-19. Moving during a pandemic, the isolation imposed by Covid-19, and the steady stream of bad news – all this has definitely made living up to the Twitter write up a challenge. But the goal is to keep trying, which is another thing about me – I'm adamant. I'm also learning to love myself for not just what I think are my strengths but also my many flaws.

You seem to have some interest in youth outreach. For instance, apart from being an invited speaker for various literary programmes organised by the likes of The Arts House, the National Museum of Singapore and Epigram Books, you speak at schools and have been a volunteer teacher to students in Phnom Penh, Cambodia, as well as a volunteer mentor with SINDA. When

reaching out to the young, what are some "big picture" messages you try to put across, given the demands of today's world?

I am lucky to have had good role models or people who were there for me as I grew up, and would like to pay it forward. We are all the products of the networks of people, opportunities and challenges that we grow up with. Obviously some of us have more or less fortunate networks than others. If I can help strengthen this network for someone else, either by being a listening ear, encouraging them or dismantling stereotypes, I feel privileged to play that role.

This is why I joined SINDA as a mentor. My main role with my mentees is first to listen. If I have a message for them or for young people who join my literary talks, it is that they are capable and should thus believe in themselves. We grow up in social and media environments that can reinforce harmful messaging, such as gender or racial stereotypes and conventions about what it means to be cool. We may even experience incidents where we are made to feel less worthy than we really are. Students who perform poorly in one exam or grow up in difficult backgrounds may come away feeling insecure. In my volunteering and writing, I hope to empower people who may feel marginalized by such incidents and discourse. I hope to show them that they can rise above it all. People generally know the technicalities of what to do but we all could do with a listening ear and some encouragement. I also encourage the young to be critical of what they read or hear, including what they hear from me, so they continue to be discerning of the messaging they receive.

Editor's Note: *For a glimpse of what Warran likes to share with the young, here is an extract from a speech he gave at his alma mater Victoria School's Student Leaders' Investiture Ceremony in 2021: "I have two messages for you. First, believe in yourself. You have gotten here mostly because the people around you believe in you, and you have seized on the opportunities they made available to become better. I hope you will spend the next year deepening your belief in yourself, your dreams, your conscience to recognise what's right, and your* *ability to act on it. Many times over the next year, you might doubt if you are good enough, or be simply overwhelmed by the workload of CCAs and lessons. You might wonder what your friends think of you, or want to copy someone else instead of just being you. Many of you have probably faced such situations already. If I was honest, I still have some of these doubts as an adult. When I first published my novel, I was really afraid of what people would think of it, and of me for having had the nerve to write one. But you will overcome. You will figure it out, if not from an instant Google search, then the inevitable algorithm of time. You will make mistakes, but you will pick yourself up. You'll be surprised at the number of people who will encourage you, and you will appreciate them for it. You will gain confidence in being yourself, beneath the trophies and the failures. You will grow as a leader and a person, and have fun along the way... My second message is to extend that same belief to others. It's easy to give orders once you don a badge. Or get flustered when someone from your baton relay team drags down everyone's timing. But I hope you will also believe in your friends. Listen to them. They might have the same fears as you, want the same sense of community as you. I've found that after making a mistake, I responded the least well when it was rubbed in my face. People usually know they've made a mistake. But I've always appreciated the friends who clapped me on my back to say it's ok, and to move on. Theirs is the faith I aspire to reciprocate. In this, I have found two values to be useful. Be thoughtful. That seconds of delay to think and respond can make a difference. And two, be kind..."*

Finally, Warran, I understand you have learnt Spanish at a certain level. What motivated you to pick up this language? What other languages are you comfortable with? How has learning languages proved useful for you as you explore different cities of the world with a sense of wonder and curiosity? Beyond languages, what have been useful for you in your own discovery of different places, peoples and practices?

I was such a nerd. During National Service, I wanted to learn a third language during the weekend so as to make the two years more productive! But I had always wanted to learn a third language and was finally able to sign myself up when I was in NS. An aunt encouraged me to study Spanish because I was interested in diplomacy and many countries have Spanish as their official language. I only belatedly realised that Singapore doesn't have embassies in Spanish-speaking countries. But I enjoy the language in its own right, be it speaking it with friends or listening to Spanish reggaetón music (big Daddy Yankee fan). Hopefully, it may one day come in useful, such as in the US or at the UN. I learned Malay as part of my posting in Kuala Lumpur with MFA. I learned Tamil growing up. I also picked up a smattering of Japanese in Tokyo.

Languages open new worlds for me to learn about and immerse myself in. It is fun speaking in different languages, and listening to their music. They are also interesting to study. With Malay, I enjoyed learning which word had come from India, the Middle-East or English, and how to create verbs or nouns out of a root word. Similarly with Spanish, there are words that are influenced by Arabic or Latin because of Spain's interactions with North Africa, Arabia and Europe. I enjoyed noticing how much more gruffly Japanese was spoken in the *dojo*, as opposed to in regular speech. Learning other languages is a way to get to know people who may not speak English or are more comfortable in their local languages. It opens up conversations and insights, especially when I am overseas. But ultimately, the main ingredients to discovering a place are an open mind, sincerity and respect. Languages can be a doorbell to ring at the door, but the person needs to be genuine and sincere before the host opens the door to let him in.

FOND MEMORIES

Picture courtesy of Warran Kalasegaran

"What I remember most about studying overseas must be time spent doing everyday things with friends. This could be catching a coffee break while studying at the library, playing drinking games and going on a night out, or having a snowfight at Leamington Park. I really enjoyed talking with my friends, from the deep conversations to the funny banter to anything in between. I also got to see parts of the world where my friends lived. I visited their homes in the UK and they brought me to climb the tor rock formations in Devonshire or row in the Thames in London. As I was learning Spanish at university, I did a homestay in Valencia one summer. I still have fond memories of arguing with my homestay family about the cruelty of bullfighting while eating up the amazing tortillas made by abuela (grandma). But it was the people that made everything special. I got to know my friends and their families better, and we became family too. Whenever my family visited, I introduced them to my friends as well. I am always happy to host my friends whenever they visit me and show them around what I boldly claim as 'my cities' – wherever I happen to be based at a particular point in time."

—Warran Kalasegaran

Lightning Source UK Ltd.
Milton Keynes UK
UKHW021159210922
409191UK00001B/36